D0575695

American
MOM

American
MOM

A CELEBRATION OF
MOTHERHOOD IN POP CULTURE

MEREDITH HALE

STERLING
New York

STERLING
New York

An Imprint of Sterling Publishing Co., Inc.
1166 Avenue of the Americas
New York, NY 10036

ISBN 978-1-4549-2905-5

Distributed in Canada by Sterling Publishing Co., Inc.,
c/o Canadian Manda Group, 664 Annette Street
Toronto, Ontario, M6S 2C8, Canada
Distributed in the United Kingdom by GMC Distribution Services
Castle Place, 166 High Street, Lewes, East Sussex, BN7 1XU, England
Distributed in Australia by NewSouth Books
45 Beach Street, Coogee, NSW 2034, Australia

For information about custom editions, special sales, and
premium and corporate purchases, please contact Sterling Special Sales
at 800-805-5489 or specialsales@sterlingpublishing.com.

Manufactured in Canada

2 4 6 8 10 9 7 5 3 1

sterlingpublishing.com

Interior design by Christine Heun and Barbara Balch
Cover design by David Ter-Avanesyan
Picture credits can be found on page 159.

To Sloane and Logan,

who taught me everything I know about being an American mom

★

And to Chris,

the best American dad I could ask for on this journey

Introduction

"Motherhood: All love begins and ends there."
—Robert Browning

The Nursery.

A LOVING MOTHER IS EVER WATCHFUL OF HER CHILDREN'S COMFORT, AND FOR THE BABY THE BEST IS NONE TOO GOOD

IVORY SOAP is used for the bath, and the little one nestles down in bed with a contented cooing that plainly shows a sense of physical well-being. Ivory Soap is so carefully made that it is selected for uses requiring a soap of extraordinary purity. It floats.

W ho is the American mom? Through the decades, she's held many roles: an angel gently guiding her children's morals, a selfless nurse caring for other mothers' sons while her own were at war, a giddy housewife stocking the kitchen with the latest groceries and appliances, a flawless supermom balancing career and family, and—in the role most of us can identify with—a hardworking, sometimes flawed, always loving parent who would do anything for her children. Because while fashions and societal expectations may change over time, one thing remains wondrously, joyfully constant—the love between a mother and her child.

This book explores the changing role of motherhood through the images and shared cultural moments that have captured it best: magazines, advertisements, greeting cards, television shows, movies, songs, and other pop culture ephemera. Inside you'll find artwork and quotes from nineteenth-century women's magazines and advice journals; propaganda posters from World Wars I and II; haunting photographs from the Great Depression; 1950s

advertisements of the "happy housewife"—who in the 1960s turned out to be not so happy; images of fierce sitcom moms from the 1980s and '90s; and profiles of today's moms, who turn to social media as they work hard—at home, the office, or both—to make their families' busy lives hang together. You'll find moms who vacuumed in pearls and heels, moms who led union protests, moms who shook up the Harlem Renaissance, moms who rocked the silver screen, and moms who lit up Broadway. Along the way, you'll also discover facts about mothers of the American presidents, who helped shape some of the greatest leaders of this country, as well as the most memorable First Ladies, who had the unenviable task of raising their children in the White House.

As I researched this book, I found that mothers' roles were shaped by the expectations of their times, which often involved a push and pull in and out of the home—especially in times of war. During

OPPOSITE A mother and her children in an 1898 Ivory Snow® advertisement. **LEFT** An American Red Cross nurse, referred to as "The Greatest Mother," comforts a boy in this World War I propaganda poster from c. 1917.

World War II there was even a national government-subsidized childcare system so that more women could work in factories to support the war effort. As women have attempted to find their identities through the decades, mothers have struggled to find balance between child-rearing and demands outside of the home, often raising the question: *Can they have it all?* Popular culture has attempted to follow women on this journey, capturing the comedy, sacrifice, and, at times, uncertainty in the march from the traditional to the modern family.

In putting this collection together, there was a seemingly endless amount of material to choose from, and many iconic publications, shows, and other cultural touchstones didn't make it into this book, although perhaps they should have. Additionally, American popular culture tends to be a portrait of a somewhat homogenous middle class; there were many other voices and experiences that tell the story of American motherhood that weren't depicted in media or advertisements. In the twenty-first century, popular culture includes increasingly diverse voices—and with social media and other online content, there are more opportunities than ever for mothers to write their own stories.

Writing this book has taught me a great deal about the fortitude, resilience, and imagination of mothers over

the decades. It's also taught me that, at its core, motherhood hasn't changed that much over time. After all, nineteenth-century moms turning to the latest advice literature and twenty-first-century moms turning to Pinterest® aren't that different from one another. We all want what's best for our children—to give them every advantage we can and be the best parents we can be. Because, in the end, that is what it means to be an American mom.

OPPOSITE, LEFT A Kool-Aid® ad from the early 1980s. OPPOSITE, RIGHT Iconic 1950s actress Donna Reed doing laundry in a still from a 1960 episode of her television show. ABOVE Many moms (and moms-to-be) work hard outside the home, too, to make their families' busy lives hang together.

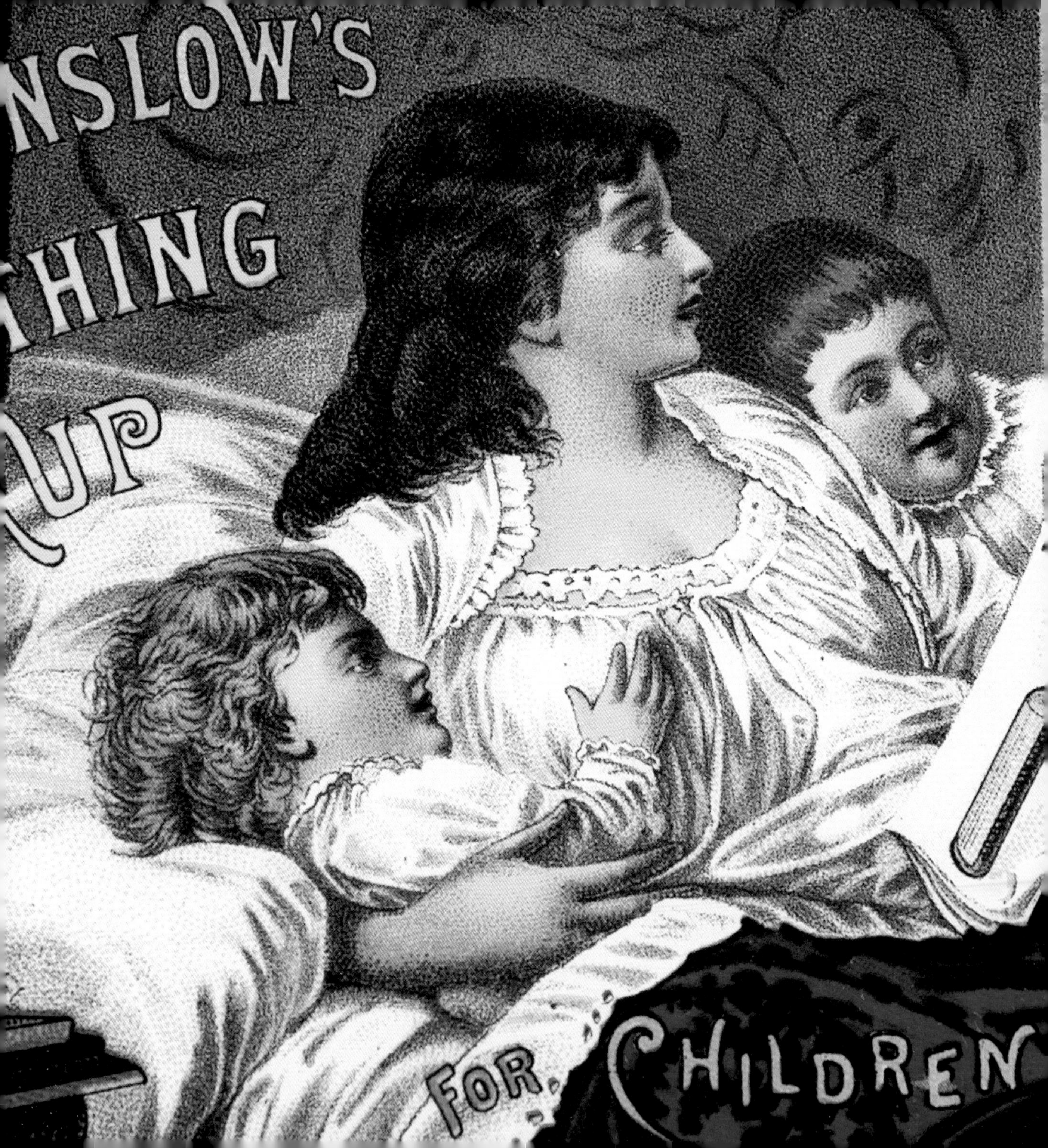

NSLOW'S
THING
UP
FOR CHILDREN

ONE

The Angel in the House

THE NINETEENTH CENTURY

"All that I am or hope to be, I owe to my angel mother."

—ABRAHAM LINCOLN

HEARTH. HOME. FAMILY. Mothers of the nineteenth century were seen as angels of the household, devoted to their husbands and tenderly guiding their children with a gentle, moral hand. With industrialization leading men away from farms and into offices and factories, women were left at home to raise the children and tend to domestic duties. Eager to raise virtuous children, mothers turned to advice books and magazines for guidance. But soon they found themselves called from those nurturing homes they so lovingly created; during the American Civil War (1861–65), mothers on both sides lent their talents to serve as nurses, seamstresses, fund-raisers, and more. America was changing as war, a growing women's rights movement, and tides of immigration swept through the country. Yet through it all, the American mom remained on a pedestal, pure and angelic in poetry, songs, and American culture.

OPPOSITE An angelic depiction of a mother embracing her children, a typical motif for nineteenth-century ads, such as this one for a popular teething remedy at the time, from 1885.

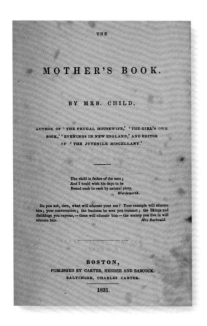

"My deepest rapture does her wrong.
Yet is it now my chosen task
To sing her worth as Maid and Wife;
Nor happier post than this I ask,
To live her laureate all my life."

—Coventry Patmore, "The Angel in the House," 1854

A Word of Advice: Women's Magazines and Advice Literature

While, for the most part, nineteenth-century moms may not have been able to vote, they were still entrusted with some pretty important tasks. After all, they were responsible for the moral and physical upbringing of the next generation. Fortunately, they had some help. The nineteenth century saw an explosion of advice literature and women's magazines guiding all aspects of the domestic realm, from sewing to raising children. Prescriptive books and journals abounded, urging moms to protect their innocent children and gently guide the development of their character. Early in the century, some works were written by members of the clergy, such as *The Mother at Home* (1833) by Reverend John S. C. Abbott. Other texts were written by women, such as abolitionist and women's rights activist Lydia Marie Child. In *The Mother's Book* (1831), Child sagely advised a mother to "govern her own feelings, and keep her heart and conscience pure." After all, children "should never be spectators of anger, or any evil passion. They come to us from heaven, with their little souls full of innocence and peace." Toward the end of the nineteenth century, literature about children's physical health, often written by pediatricians, became popular as mothers began to seek more scientific approaches to child-rearing.

GODEY'S FASHIONS FOR MAY 1862.

Popular magazines of the time included *Godey's Lady's Book* (published 1830–98) and *Peterson's Magazine* (1842–98). *Godey's*, shaped by editor Sarah Josepha Hale, was especially popular in the nineteenth century, with 150,000 subscribers by 1860. *Godey's* promoted a more traditional, Victorian view of motherhood. In addition to fashion plates and sentimental stories, the magazine offered women advice on motherhood and marriage, stressing the mother's responsibility to influence her children's religious and moral character. As one article from 1835 stated, "A pious, intelligent, and faithful mother is the greatest earthly blessing that a merciful providence can bestow on a child."

Sarah Josepha Hale (1788–1879)

Sarah Josepha Hale was the editor of *Godey's Lady's Book* from 1837 to 1877, and, under her stewardship, the publication became one of the most popular of its day. Born in Newport, New Hampshire, in 1788, Hale was homeschooled by her mother and her Dartmouth-educated brother. She became a schoolteacher and a respected author, best known for her collection of children's poetry that included "Mary Had a Little Lamb." As editor of *Godey's*, she was a passionate advocate of women's education. Hale believed a woman should have the same educational opportunities as a man—not to usurp the role of men, but to better influence the morals and piety of those around her.

Hale was socially conservative and did not support women's suffrage, believing a woman's calling was to "silently" use her moral influence upon men. Known as the "Godmother of Thanksgiving," she spent almost twenty years advocating for the creation of a national Thanksgiving holiday; it was eventually proclaimed by President Lincoln in 1863. A widow and mother of five children, Sarah Hale retired from *Godey's* in 1877 at the age of eighty-nine. She died shortly thereafter in 1879.

"God has given to man authority,
to woman influence."

—*Sarah Josepha Hale*

THE SISTER OF CHARITY

HOME TIDINGS

From Hearth to Hospital: The Civil War

Before the Civil War, mothers in America were celebrated in the home, as the country revered the virtuous and delicate "cult of true womanhood" that romanticized their domestic roles. But the ravages of war blurred the line between the public and domestic spheres, as thousands of women participated in the war effort, in both the North and South. Whether sewing uniforms, canning vegetables, or nursing fallen soldiers back to health, women were called into public service in ways they hadn't been before in America.

Union women worked in ladies'-aid societies, knitting and laundering clothing, planting gardens, raising money for supplies, and more. With their husbands and sons gone to battle, many women aided in the war effort by nursing wounded soldiers. Perhaps one of the most famous mother-nurses was Mary Ann Bickerdyke, born Mary Ann Ball in Knox County, Ohio, in 1817. A widowed mother of two sons, she studied botanical medicine and found her calling

Mrs. Margaret "Marmee" March,
Little Women

Perhaps no fictional character immortalizes the struggling yet devoted Civil War mother like Mrs. March, affectionately nicknamed "Marmee" by her daughters, in Louisa May Alcott's *Little Women* (published in 1868–69). Faced with raising four girls while her husband serves as a Union chaplain in the Civil War, Marmee is patient, involved in charity, and always a source of comfort to her children—even as they struggle financially without their male head of household for much of the novel. Embodying the virtue and good moral influence of the nineteenth-century wife and mother while wielding the strength and fortitude demanded of women during the Civil War, she was a character who truly epitomized her time.

> "The love, respect, and confidence of my children was the sweetest reward I could receive for my efforts to be the woman I would have them copy."
>
> —"Marmee" March in Louisa May Alcott's
> Little Women, 1868–69

during the Civil War. After learning of the conditions at the hospitals and camps in Cairo, Illinois, Bickerdyke went there to deliver money and supplies from her local congregation in Galesburg, Illinois—and stayed to sanitize tents and create a makeshift hospital. In the years that followed, the highly respected "Mother Bickerdyke" continued to work with the Union army, establishing more than three hundred field hospitals, serving as chief of nursing under General Ulysses S. Grant, and accompanying the forces of General Sherman during the famous "March to the Sea" through Georgia in late 1864.

In the Confederacy, women also contributed through local aid societies, providing necessities and often working as untrained nurses in their homes, as houses and churches became makeshift hospitals. Many enslaved mothers in the South fled with their families when Union troops arrived, some ending up with their children in "contraband" camps—temporary settlement camps near Union armies. With African American men often joining the Union army, life for mothers in these camps was difficult and sometimes dangerous, with low wages and a scarcity of food and supplies. But they also provided a transition to freedom. Camp residents supported the Union war effort and children attended schools established by missionaries and other groups. At the Grand Contraband Camp in Virginia, the American Missionary Association hired its first black teacher, Mary Peake, who taught dozens of students, including her own five-year-old daughter, under a tree later known as the Emancipation Oak.

In both the North and South, with fathers and husbands at war, women of all circumstances had greater responsibilities and often a much greater workload as they struggled to keep farms running, children cared for, and families fed and situated. Mothers on both sides faced enormous losses and worried for their sons on the front lines. Sarah Brandon, the Ohio mother of twenty-three children—twenty-two of them boys—became nicknamed the "Mother of the Civil War" as sixteen of her sons saw service in the war, fourteen in the Union and two in the Confederacy.

OPPOSITE The frontispiece to a 1915 edition of Louisa May Alcott's *Little Women* by acclaimed illustrator Jessie Willcox Smith. ABOVE An engraving depicting African American soldiers reuniting with loved ones mustering out of the Union Army at Little Rock, Arkansas, in 1866 after the Civil War.

"Just Before the Battle, Mother"

Song written in 1863 by American songwriter George F. Root, popular with the Union troops during the Civil War:

"Just before the battle, Mother, I am thinking most of you.
While upon the field we're watching, with the enemy in view.
Comrades brave are 'round me lying, filled with thoughts of home and God;
For well they know that on the morrow, some will sleep beneath the sod.

"Farewell, Mother, you may never press me to your breast again;
But, oh, you'll not forget me, Mother, if I'm numbered with the slain.
Oh, I long to see you, Mother, and the loving ones at home,
But I'll never leave our banner till in honor I can come. . . .

"Hark! I hear the bugles sounding, 'tis the signal for the fight,
Now, may God protect us, Mother, as He ever does the right.
Hear 'The Battle Cry of Freedom,' how it swells upon the air,
Oh, yes, we'll rally 'round the standard, or we'll nobly perish there. . . ."

"And Oh! let not the appeal of a Mother's Grief be
in Vain. . . . Hoping the Prayer of a Mother may
be heard through you and my Son restored to me."

—Amanda A. Promie of Philadelphia
in a letter to President Lincoln, June 1864

Celebrating Mom: The Mother of Mother's Day

Many people are familiar with Anna Marie Jarvis, the founder of Mother's Day, which was first proclaimed a US holiday by President Woodrow Wilson in 1914, "as a public expression of love and reverence for the mothers of our country." But the inspiration behind Mother's Day actually goes back further in time, to the Civil War, with Jarvis's own mother, the ever-industrious Ann Reeves Jarvis.

In the 1850s, wanting to help lower mortality rates among children in her local area of West Virginia, Ann organized Mother's Day Work Clubs to combat contamination and unsanitary conditions, teaching mothers the importance of boiling water and protecting milk and food from spoilage. Sadly, Ann Jarvis lost many of her own children to childhood diseases common in Appalachia, which inspired her efforts to improve conditions for other children and bring medicine to poor families. When the Civil War began, Ann's clubs shifted their focus to feeding and clothing both Union and Confederate soldiers, doggedly remaining neutral to help all in need. Ann maintained this neutrality after the war, staging a Mother's Friendship Day picnic to help heal a deeply divided community.

When Ann Reeves Jarvis died in 1905, her daughter Anna devoted herself to establishing a day to celebrate mothers. Today, Mother's Day is a cherished—and profitable—holiday. In 2017, the National Retail Federation expected Mother's Day spending to reach a historic high of $23.6 billion. Apparently, when it comes to celebrating Mom, Americans spare no expense.

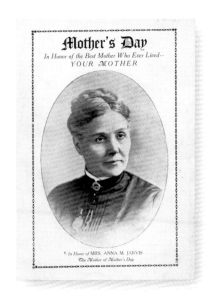

OPPOSITE Cover of the sheet music for "Just Before the Battle, Mother" by George F. Root.
LEFT Early Mother's Day card, c. 1920
ABOVE Cover of an early twentieth-century program for a service honoring Anna Jarvis, the founder of Mother's Day.

BY THE NUMBERS
According to Hallmark®, around 133 million Mother's Day cards are exchanged annually.

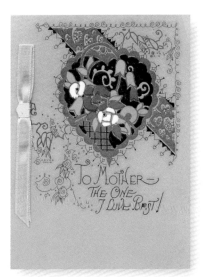

Home for the Holidays

There's no place like home for the holidays—especially if you're celebrating with Mom. Moms have been commemorated in holiday postcards, greeting cards, and magazines for as long as Americans have been spreading Christmas cheer in print. Holiday cards hold a special place in Americans' hearts, going back to the first Christmas card produced in the United States (by lithographer Louis Prang) in 1875. Christmas cards began to grow in popularity with the founding of Hallmark in 1910, and the purchasing and exchanging of cards gradually expanded to other holidays as well. But it was in the 1940s and '50s that holiday cards hit their stride, as Hallmark commissioned artwork for its cards by extraordinary artists such as Norman Rockwell, Grandma Moses, and Salvador Dali. Norman Rockwell especially captured the joy of the American mom and her family in their celebrations, as he and other artists portrayed these festive images on cards and paintings and in other media.

Whether gracing the cover of a greeting card or the *Saturday Evening Post*, holiday images of Mom, home, and family have brightened the mailboxes and coffee tables of Americans for generations—and continue to warm our hearts today, no matter what holiday you celebrate.

May your
Christmas Day be bright,
With the Season's great delight
As the ruddy firelight's glow
Brings back thoughts of long ago.

OPPOSITE An illustration from *Puck* magazine featuring a happy extended family celebrating Christmas, December 8, 1897. **LEFT** A mother and child cuddle before the "ruddy firelight" on this Christmas card from c. 1910. **ABOVE** Thanksgiving dinner, cooked by Mom; cover of *Collier's* magazine illustrated by Edward Penfield, c. 1880.

TWO

The Art of Motherhood

THE PRE-WAR YEARS

"The hand that rocks the cradle is the hand that rules the world."
—WILLIAM ROSS WALLACE, EPONYMOUS POEM, 1865

A NEW CENTURY EMERGED in 1900, and with it, new roles for the American mom. Mothers often became involved in women's clubs, or organizations such as the National Congress of Mothers (later the National Parent Teacher Association, or PTA). There were increased educational opportunities for women, and the idea of a "New Woman" emerged—the educated feminist with a more independent spirit. The consummate New Woman, the Gibson Girl, began appearing in print, capturing the nation's imagination. At the same time, women subscribed to magazines in record numbers, and publishers hired talented female illustrators who brought American motherhood to life through their unique perspectives. Amidst a backdrop of a rising suffragette movement and the specter of war, the early twentieth-century mom nurtured her children and remained the center of the family home.

OPPOSITE Detail of *Supper,* by Jessie Willcox Smith, from a series of illustrations she did entitled "A Mother's Day" for *Scribner's* magazine, December 1902.

Through Her Eyes

Female magazine readership was thriving at the turn of the century. Between 1885 and 1905, there were around eleven thousand magazines and periodicals published in the United States—and about 88 percent of the subscribers were women. And who better to capture the magic

> "The new woman . . . has come to stay. . . . The sufferings of the past have but strengthened her, maternity has deepened her, education is broadening her—and she now knows that she must perfect herself if she would . . . leave her imprint upon immortality."
>
> —*Winnifred Harper Cooley,*
> The New Womanhood, *1904*

of their day-to-day experiences than other women? Many female illustrators made a name for themselves at the turn of the century, bringing some of the most enduring images of motherhood to the pages of magazines and literature.

Three well-known artists who lived and worked together—Jessie Willcox Smith, Violet Oakley, and Elizabeth Shippen Green—became known as the "Red Rose Girls," after the inn they rented in the suburb of Villanova outside of Philadelphia. (They received this nickname from noted American illustrator Howard Pyle, with whom they studied at Philadelphia's Drexel Institute of Art, Science, and Industry.) Described as "romantic realism," their art graced the pages of *Harper's Magazine*, works of literature, and even public murals. Violet Oakley was the principal artist for numerous murals that grace the Pennsylvania Capitol.

But it was the work of Jessie Willcox Smith—ironically never a mother herself—that truly captured the powerful bonds between mothers and children. From sentimental ads for Ivory Soap® to her covers for *Good Housekeeping* and illustrations for children's books such as *Little Women* and *Heidi*, Smith's keen eye brought to life the magic of childhood and the tender moments between mothers and their children. Often capturing quiet, domestic moments, such as mothers reading to or bathing their children, her work portrayed the day-to-day devotion of motherhood in loving scenes that still inspire readers today.

OPPOSITE Detail of *Life Was Made for Love and Cheer*, a watercolor painted by Elizabeth Shippen Green in 1904, depicts Green, her fellow artists Jessie Willcox Smith and Violet Oakley, and their family and friends at the Red Rose Inn in Villanova.

Jessie Willcox Smith (1863–1935)

Jessie Willcox Smith was born in Philadelphia, Pennsylvania. Trained as a teacher, she briefly taught kindergarten before deciding to pursue art. She attended the Philadelphia School of Design for Women (present-day Moore College of Art & Design) and the Pennsylvania Academy of the Fine Arts in Philadelphia, where she studied with famed American realist Thomas Eakins. Upon graduation, she went to work at the *Ladies' Home Journal* and took classes at the Drexel Institute of Art, Science, and Industry (present-day Drexel University). There she met the other "Red Rose Girls"—Elizabeth Shippen Green and Violet Oakley. The three women lived and worked together and became some of the most successful female artists of the "Golden Age of Illustration."

A prolific illustrator, Smith's work was published in *Harper's Weekly*, *Harper's Bazaar*, *Scribner's*, *Collier's*, and more. She famously created a series of Mother Goose illustrations for *Good Housekeeping*—a magazine for which she created almost two hundred illustrations. In 1991, Smith became the second woman to be inducted into the Hall of Fame of the Society of Illustrators in New York.

"In every age the greatest artists have spent themselves in efforts to express the poetry in the relation between mother and child."

—*"Mother-Love in Jessie Willcox Smith's Art,"*
Current Literature *magazine, 1908*

OPPOSITE Portrait of Jessie Willcox Smith, 1917. LEFT Cover of *The Jessie Willcox Smith Mother Goose*, 1914. BELOW Detail of *Morning*, Jessie Willcox Smith, from a series of illustrations she did entitled "A Mother's Day" for *Scribner's* magazine, December 1902.

FUN FACT Books illustrated by Jessie Willcox Smith include Henry Wadsworth Longfellow's *Evangeline* (1897 edition, co-illustrated with Violet Oakley), Robert Louis Stevenson's *A Child's Garden of Verses* (1905 edition), Louisa May Alcott's *Little Women* (1915 edition), and Johanna Spyri's *Heidi* (1922 edition).

RIGHT An illustration by Smith for a 1905 edition of Robert Louis Stevenson's collection *A Child's Garden of Verses*, 1885.

OPPOSITE Two covers by Smith for *Good Housekeeping* from September 1910 and December 1914.

"Certainly no other artist is so fitted . . . to make for us pictures so truly an index to what we as a magazine are striving for. . . . The highest ideals of the American home, the home with that certain sweet wholesomeness one associates with a sunny living-room—and children."

—Good Housekeeping *note on Jessie Willcox Smith's covers for the magazine, 1918*

"M-O-T-H-E-R (A Word That Means the World to Me)"

Perhaps the most recognizable of early musical tributes to mom is "M-O-T-H-E-R (A Word That Means the World to Me)," by Howard Johnson and Theodore Morse, made famous by iconic singer and vaudeville star Eva Tanguay in 1915. A sentimental favorite, the song was also performed by other artists of the time, including Sophie Tucker, Henry Burr, and George W. Ballard. The first verse follows:

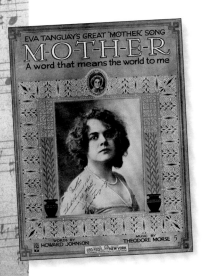

"I've been around the world, you bet, but never went to school,
  Hard knocks are all I seem to get, perhaps I've been a fool;
  But still, some educated folks, supposed to be so swell,
  Would fail if they were called upon a simple word to spell.
  Now if you'd like to put me to a test,
  There's one dear name that I can spell the best:
  M is for the million things she gave me,
  O means only that she's growing old,
  T is for the tears she shed to save me,
  H is for her heart of purest gold,
  E is for her eyes with love-light shining,
  R means right, and right she'll always be,
  Put them all together, they spell *MOTHER*,
  A word that means the world to me."

"A mother is the truest friend we have."

—*Washington Irving*

Singing Mom's Praises

In the early twentieth century, musicians looking to please the masses could always fall back on one surefire subject: dear old Mom. An abundance of sheet music was published featuring sentimental songs about Mom, often accompanied by illustrated cover art. There were endless variations on the theme, with titles such as "That Old Irish Mother of Mine," "My Mother's Rosary," "My Yiddishe Momme," "Paint Me a Picture of Mama," "Mother, Sweet Mother," "That Old Fashioned Mother of Mine," and many, many more. While today such songs have gone out of style, back then there was no shortage of odes to a mother's love and devotion.

Such songs became especially popular around times of war as soldiers grew nostalgic for the familiarity and comfort of home. As a soldier laments in the 1863 ballad "Who Will Care for Mother Now?":

"Soon with angels I'll be marching, With bright laurels on my brow; I have for my country fallen, Who will care for mother now?"

And in the lyrics of the popular 1917 tune "So Long, Mother," a soldier fighting in World War I croons, "So long my dear old lady, Don't you cry, Just kiss your grown-up baby good-bye, Somewhere in France I'll be dreaming of you."

While many of these songs have been forgotten over the years, a few remain relatively well known. The famous Irish ballad "Mother Machree" was written in 1910 by Rida Johnson Young, with music by Chauncey Olcott and Ernest R. Ball, for the musical *Barry of Ballymore*. The touching song, sung by musicians over the years including John McDermott and Connie Francis, declares "I love the dear silver that shines in your hair, And the brow that's all furrowed and wrinkled with care. I kiss the dear fingers so toil-worn for me, Oh, God bless you and keep you, Mother Machree!"

OPPOSITE Singer Eva Tanguay featured on the 1915 sheet music cover of "M-O-T-H-E-R (A Word That Means the World to Me)." ABOVE "Who Will Care for Mother Now?" sheet music cover.

FUN FACT The song "M-O-T-H-E-R (A Word That Means the World to Me)" was used in the 1947 movie *Mother Wore Tights*, starring Betty Grable and Dan Dailey.

Mama's Little Girl

Mothers and daughters. This special, complex bond has been portrayed in many ways over the years, from the idealized Mrs. March and her adoring daughters in *Little Women* (see page 6), to the alternately guilt-ridden and scheming relationship between Joan Crawford and Ann Blyth in the film *Mildred Pierce* (1945, based on the 1941 novel by James M. Cain), to the challenging love between rebellious Merida and her mama bear, Queen Elinor, in the animated film *Brave* (2012), to the fast-talking, caffeine-fueled friendship between Lorelai and Rory in the hit TV show *Gilmore Girls* (2000–2007). Pick up a magazine, turn on the television, or peruse the pages of a novel, and you'll discover mothers and daughters who share each other's spirit while breaking each other's hearts, who cry easily and laugh fiercely (often in the same argument), and who forgive and support each other in the face of whatever life throws at them.

It's a common saying that daughters turn into their mothers. In pop culture, that's often true—literally. In the mid-twentieth century, American artist Al Parker illustrated thirty covers for *Ladies' Home Journal* featuring mothers and daughters in

"What do girls do who haven't any mothers
to help them through their troubles?"

—*Louisa May Alcott*

matching outfits, a colorful statement that soon became a fashion trend, as stores started selling mother-daughter matching dresses and dress patterns. Film took this theme one step further, with mothers and daughters actually trading places. Turn on the 1976 film *Freaky Friday* (or any of its remakes), and watch mother-daughter duo Barbara Harris and Jodie Foster switch bodies for some real mother-daughter bonding.

Mother-daughter relationships are often full of drama. But beneath this drama lies one of the deepest loves imaginable—a devotion honored and celebrated on the pages of scripts, novels, and poetry throughout generations. Because as complicated as it may be, the profound love between a mother and her daughter is one of enduring strength, resilience, and beauty.

OPPOSITE, LEFT Colorized still of mother-daughter pair Joan Crawford and Ann Blyth in *Mildred Pierce*, 1945. **OPPOSITE, RIGHT** *Ladies' Home Journal* cover from June 1948, illustrated by Al Parker, featuring mother and daughter in matching swimsuits. **ABOVE** Lauren Graham and Alexis Bledel as mother-daughter duo Lorelai and Rory Gilmore in *Gilmore Girls*.

THREE

The Greatest Mother in the World

WORLD WAR I

"Make your Mother proud of you, and to Liberty be true."
—George M. Cohan, "Over There," 1917

APRIL 1917 WAS a turning point in American history. After a series of hostile actions by the Germans in the previous months, President Woodrow Wilson reversed his platform of American neutrality. On April 2, he asked Congress to declare war on Germany; four days later, the United States joined the Allies and entered World War I, already in its third year. From that moment forward, life on the home front was one of change. With so many men at war—more than four million—women found themselves needed in the workforce, both to help with positions normally filled by men and to fill new roles created by the war. Government-issued propaganda posters urged mothers to buy war bonds, while the Red Cross encouraged mothers to aid in the war effort by knitting goods and organizing food and supplies.

OPPOSITE A detail from one of many American Red Cross posters depicting the "Greatest Mother" comforting a child; this one is from 1917.

Popular women's magazines imparted to housewives the importance of rationing at home, suggesting they cut back where possible as well as plant vegetable gardens and can food. In a time of war unlike any the world had ever seen before, American mothers faced new challenges and served their country in extraordinary ways.

> ## "How a Woman Can Help
> *First:* herself. *Second:* her children and her children's children.
> *Third:* her nation, whose flag protects her and all whom she loves.
> She Can Own a U.S. Liberty Bond"
>
> —*From an ad in* Ladies' Home Journal, *November 1917*

Uncle Sam Wants Mom!

Entire books have been written recounting the courage and sacrifice of the American soldier during World War I. But back home there was another important story taking place. This quieter, less trumpeted narrative involved women and mothers, who found themselves suddenly called to service in vital ways. To help fund the war, the US government borrowed nearly $22 billion from American citizens through the sale of Liberty Bonds. How did the government raise so much money? In part, with the help of mothers. The newly formed Committee on Public Information found an effective way to reach the public—with propaganda posters featuring heartfelt, impossible-to-ignore images of mothers pleading with Americans to support the war effort by purchasing bonds. In fact, the Division of Pictorial Publicity, under the

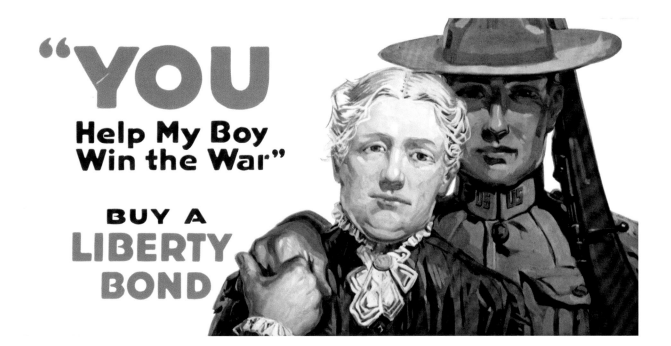

"YOU Help My Boy Win the War"

BUY A LIBERTY BOND

leadership of famous American illustrator Charles Dana Gibson, found many uses for Mom in posters—including urging sons to enlist, imploring fellow mothers to ration valuable food supplies, and asking women to actively support the American Red Cross.

The Red Cross also reached out to women through advertisements. In popular women's magazines, the Red Cross instructed readers on how to sew pillowcases, washcloths, and bandages for the troops, as well as how to gather or create other supplies.

OPPOSITE, TOP A US Food Administration poster from 1918, advocating for housewives to plant vegetable gardens as well as to can and dry their produce. OPPOSITE, BOTTOM A Red Cross recruitment poster urging moms to pick up their knitting needles, c. 1918. ABOVE A Liberty Bond appeal featuring a mother and her soldier son, 1917. RIGHT An antiwaste campaign poster by famed illustrator Charles Dana Gibson for the government's Division of Pictorial Publicity, May 1918.

> # "The American housewife is to-day a more important factor in our nation's welfare than ever before."
>
> —*"The Woman and the War,"* Ladies' Home Journal, *July 1917*

Women who wanted to participate even more directly were encouraged to serve as nurses. While, at least in the early days of the war, nurses were required to be unmarried, Red Cross posters still tapped into women's maternal instincts. Advertisements urged women to serve as the "Greatest Mother in the World" overseas, featuring images of women sheltering children and cradling fallen soldiers—oceans away from their own loving mothers' arms. Indeed, during the war, all women had the opportunity to serve their country, by nobly serving as mothers to all.

Yet one of the biggest ways the government urged mothers to participate in the war effort was at the kitchen table. To respond to the growing food shortages in Europe, Herbert Hoover, then head of the US Food Administration, urged Americans to conserve wheat and other food products so more could be sent overseas. As mothers were usually the ones who shopped for and planned their families' meals, much of this responsibility fell to them. American housewives signed patriotic pledges to cut back and soon found themselves participating in "wheatless Mondays," "meatless Tuesdays," and "porkless Saturdays." The July 1917 issue of the *Ladies' Home Journal* ran a special section titled "The Woman and the War," which featured articles such as "What Is It That I Waste?," "The Garden You Can Plant Now," and "Meatless-Day Dishes by Englishwomen That Are Just as Good Here." The Food Administration proclaimed that "Food Will Win the War"—and in that battle, American moms were on the front line.

HERBERT HOOVER
Food Administrator

IT IS through the use of such dishes as these, the recipes for which have been approved, that every American household can contribute much to the necessary saving of wheat.

United States Food Administration.

CORN DUMPLINGS. Make a stew from a cheap cut of meat cut into small pieces, with the desired amount of carrots, onions and potatoes. Pour enough boiling water over a cupful of corn meal to make a soft dough; let cool; then mix in one cupful of flour sieved with two teaspoonfuls of baking powder; add one egg, and mix thoroughly; form into small round balls and put them into the stew for the last twenty-five minutes of cooking. Dish up on a hot platter, pour the gravy over all and arrange the dumplings around on a border. These will take the place of bread at the meal. These corn dumplings are especially nice served with chicken potpie accompanied by either jelly or a relish.

CONTRIBUTED BY HARRIET COATES

The New Cereal Dishes

For Luncheons and Dinners

WE ARE rather apt to think of cereals as breakfast foods only, served with sugar, cream or fruit, hardly placing bread in its different forms in the same class of foods. When it is desired to use little bread at dinner the nutritive elements found in flour baked into bread may be supplied by combining the coarser cereals, or ground meals made from them, into wholesome, appetizing and thoroughly satisfying dishes. In our sparing use of meat we could well go back to the hearty dumpling stews that seem to be lightly esteemed by the average housewife. The left-over cereal from breakfast may be so happily used as to seem like a first appearance when made into delicious nourishing puddings with fruit.

SALTED CODFISH AND EGG NOODLES. Boil a sufficient amount of egg noodles, made of half rye and half white flour, in salted water; drain thoroughly, and put them into an open fireproof casserole. Shape into a border around the dish. Fill up the center with pieces of cold boiled salted codfish; pour over a thick white sauce; garnish the top with strips of canned pimientos. Put in a hot oven for fifteen minutes. Serve hot.

CONTRIBUTED BY HARRIET COATES

CHICKEN TART À LA POMPADOUR. This dish of spaghetti and chicken has a history, as it was invented for the Marquise de Pompadour. Boil a pound of spaghetti, taking care not to break it. Drain thoroughly and use it to line a well-greased mold, twisting the spaghetti round and round. Fill the center with a mixture composed of three cupfuls of cold chopped chicken, three-quarters of a cupful of cream thickened with flour, a piece of butter substituted with the yolk of an egg, seasoned with salt, pepper and a sprinkling of nutmeg. Steam for one hour, turn out on a dish and surround with tomato sauce.

CONTRIBUTED BY HARRIET COATES

MACARONI AND MEAT HASH. Boil a quarter of a pound of macaroni; drain, and put it into a buttered casserole, adding a little clarified sausage fat. Push the macaroni to the sides of the dish and add a sprinkling of grated cheese. Fill the center with chopped cooked meat of any kind, with which a little sausage has been mixed. Moisten with meat stock. Place in the oven until hot throughout. Serve in the casserole.

CONTRIBUTED BY HARRIET COATES

MOCK RAREBIT WITH OATMEAL. Cook as usual two cupfuls of oatmeal or rolled oats; just before serving add one cupful of soft, mild, grated cheese, one tablespoonful of butter and one level teaspoonful of salt. Stir until the cheese is melted and thoroughly blended.

CONTRIBUTED BY HARRIET COATES

CEREAL PANCAKES. Put two cupfuls of cold cooked cereal into a mixing bowl; mash fine with a fork to free from lumps; add two tablespoonfuls of sugar, a quarter of a teaspoonful of salt, one well-beaten egg and a cupful of milk. Sieve two cupfuls of flour with two teaspoonfuls of baking powder. Stir into the mixture and beat thoroughly to a smooth batter. Fry in large pancakes on a hot well-greased griddle and spread with jelly. Pile one on top of another and, in serving, cut as you would a pie.

CONTRIBUTED BY HARRIET COATES

RICE ENTRÉE WITH TOMATOES. Cook half a cupful of rice and three-quarters of a cupful of stewed tomatoes in one cupful of broth (or stock may be used instead) until the rice is tender. Use a double boiler for the purpose, and remove the cover after the rice is cooked if there is too much liquid remaining in the boiler. Stir in three tablespoonfuls of chicken fat with a fork so the rice may remain unbroken.

CONTRIBUTED BY HARRIET COATES

CEREAL OMELET. Beat the yolks of two eggs until they are lemon colored; add two tablespoonfuls of hot water and a little salt and pepper; whip the whites of the eggs to a stiff froth and fold them lightly into the yolks; pour the mixture into a greased omelet or frying pan and cook slowly until it is brown on the under side. Have ready half a cupful of any cold cooked cereal that has been seasoned with salt, pepper, a chopped onion and one teaspoonful of melted bacon or suet fat; spread the cereal over the top of the omelet, fold over and turn out on a hot platter. Garnish with parsley. It should be served at once. The onion may be omitted from the omelet, and the cereal may be sweetened with honey if preferred; or jelly or stewed raisins may be used to make it a sweet omelet if desired.

SCALLOPED FISH AND HOMINY. Place flaked pieces of canned salmon in the center of a baking dish; take some boiled hominy and shape it into a border around the dish; pour over a white sauce, sprinkle the hominy with bread crumbs and the fish with minced parsley and bake in a hot oven until nicely browned. Serve hot in the same dish in which it was cooked. Rice or macaroni may be used in place of hominy and minced left-over meat in place of the fish.

DATE HOMINY PUDDING. Soak one cupful of hominy in four cupfuls of water with one teaspoonful of salt overnight. Simmer in the same water until the liquid is absorbed, then stir in a cupful of sugar, a grating of nutmeg and the grated rind of one lemon. Grease a pudding mold and in the bottom place four dates. Cover with an inch-thick layer of hominy. Arrange the remaining dates around the sides of the mold; add enough hominy by spoonfuls to hold them in place, then pour in the remainder, cover and steam for two hours. When done, unmold and serve cold with cream and sugar or hot with a sweet sauce.

CORN-MEAL PUDDING WITH APRICOTS. Pour three cupfuls of scalding hot milk on one cupful of sifted corn meal; stir in two tablespoonfuls of sugar, one teaspoonful of powdered ginger and half a teaspoonful of salt. Now add six apricots, canned, sliced thin. Bake for one hour and a half in a moderate oven. Garnish with sliced apricots and serve with sauce made from the juice of the apricots.

CONTRIBUTED BY MARION HARRIS NEIL

FRUITED CEREAL MOLDS. Wash half a pound of prunes and soak them overnight. Simmer in the same water until tender, adding one lemon, sliced, one stick of cinnamon and a quarter of a cupful of sugar when nearly done. Let stand until cold; strain off the liquid, and pit the prunes. Put aside one for each mold and cut the remainder fine, removing most of the skin. Soften one rounded teaspoonful of gelatin in one tablespoonful of cold prune juice and dissolve in one tablespoonful of boiling juice. Mix thoroughly with the prune pulp. Have ready two cupfuls of oatmeal that has been cooked with one teaspoonful of salt in four cupfuls of water. Rinse the molds in cold water and fill with the oatmeal and prune pulp, placing the lattey in the center. Serve very cold with sugar and cream, decorated with the whole prunes.

CONTRIBUTED BY WINNIFRED FALES

Digitized by   Original from

OPPOSITE, TOP "The Greatest Mother in the World" poster, 1917. OPPOSITE, BOTTOM A mother cradling a child—superimposed over an American flag—hovers above troops, in this 1918 Liberty Loan committee poster. LEFT A page from the November 1917 issue of the *Ladies' Home Journal*, with cooking tips for incorporating oats, hominy, and other nonwheat cereals into lunch and dinner dishes—with a helpful note from Herbert Hoover on the necessity of saving wheat.

BY THE NUMBERS Many war posters urged civilians to "Eat less wheat, meat, sugar and fats to save for the army and our allies." The campaign worked; according to the National Archives, by 1918 the United States was exporting three times as much breadstuffs, meat, and sugar as it had prior to World War I.

Blue and Gold Star Mothers

The star as a symbol of military service dates back to World War I, when US Army Captain Robert Queisser of the 5th Ohio Infantry designed the Blue Star service flag in honor of his sons fighting in the war. It quickly became used by families to indicate a child serving in the military. Shortly afterward, it became customary when a son died in combat to hang a gold star flag in his honor. Following this tradition, in 1918, President Wilson approved a suggestion from the Women's Committee of the Council of National Defense that mourning American women wear a black band on their left arm with a gold star for each family member who died in service. One of the most moving songs from World War I was titled "There's a Little Blue Star in the Window (And It Means All the World to Me)" from 1918. Lyrics were by Paul B. Armstrong and music was by R. Henri Klickmann. The main chorus follows:

There are stars in the high heavens shining
With a promise of hope in their light.
There are stars in the field of Old Glory,
The emblem of honor and Right.
But no star ever shone with more brightness, I know,
Than the one for my boy o'er the sea.
There's a little blue star in the window,
And it means all the world to me.

On June 4, 1928, the organization American Gold Star Mothers—founded by Grace Darling Seibold, who lost her son George in the war—was formally established in Washington, DC.

During World War II, three hundred mothers of servicemen met in Flint, Michigan, and the Blue Star Mothers of America was born. In June 1960, the organization was chartered by Congress. Over the years, Blue Star Mothers have provided one another with support, worked in hospitals, volunteered with veterans, and much more.

Today we continue to honor the courage and sacrifice of mothers whose sons and daughters are actively serving or who have given their lives for their country. Gold Star Mother's Day is observed in the United States on the last Sunday in September, in honor of Gold Star mothers.

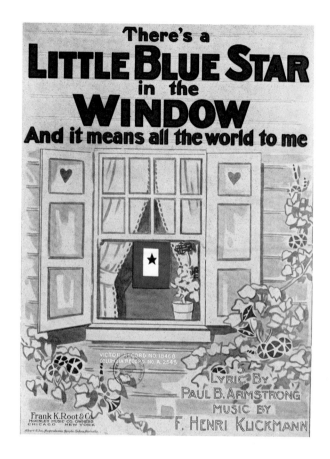

OPPOSITE, TOP A group of early Gold Star mothers gathers at the Tomb of the Unknown Soldier at Arlington National Cemetery in 1925; the American Gold Star Mothers organization was formally founded by Grace Darling Seibold three years later. OPPOSITE, BOTTOM Three-cent stamp issued in 1948 commemorating Gold Star Mothers. ABOVE Cover of sheet music for "There's a Little Blue Star in the Window (And It Means All the World to Me)," 1918.

> "Women enlist now and help the farmer fight the food famine."
>
> —*Woman's Land Army poster slogan, 1918*

Women at Work

With their husbands and sons at war in Europe, many American women entered the workforce in new ways. Women worked in factories as punch-press operators, grinders, riveting-machine operators, inspectors, crane operators, assemblers, case makers, and more. According to the Social Security Administration, at the close of World War I, women constituted around 20 percent of the workforce in all manufacturing industries in the United States.

But women's work wasn't limited to factories; they also filled traditionally male jobs such as bank tellers, elevator operators, streetcar conductors, and other uncustomary roles. There was also heavy demand for stenographers, telegraphers, and phone operators to work for the government, the railroads, and other industries. And, with their husbands and sons at war, many women joined the Women's Land Army of America, running farms and producing food and goods for the war effort.

BY THE NUMBERS In 1918, nearly three million new female workers were employed in the food, textile, and war-related industries.

OPPOSITE A group of women at work in the welding department of the Lincoln Motor Company in Detroit, Michigan. **ABOVE, RIGHT** A poster from 1918 advertising a training school for the Woman's Land Army of America at the University of Virginia in Richmond.

Which One of These Jobs Can You Fill?

The Time May Soon Come When You Will Have to Choose

There May be a Great Demand for Car Conductors

Women are Working in the American Railroad Shops

These New York Girls are Excellent Carpenters

A Woman Engineer Oiling Up a Factory Engine

English Railroads Now Use Women "Trainmen"

An Expert Electrician Who Has Applied for Membership in the Electrical Union

A Good Boot Repairer

An Expert Barber

Wireless Operators Will be in Great Demand. Why do You Not Join a Class Now?

Women are Already Running Elevators in Hotels and Office Buildings

ABOVE A page from the August 1917 issue of the *Ladies' Home Journal* depicting the many types of jobs women could look to fill during World War I, including pilot, signal operator, taxicab driver, meter reader, dairy woman, electrician, and boot repairer. **OPPOSITE** Janet "Jessie" Woodrow Wilson, c. 1850.

Without formalized childcare (which would come later, during World War II), mothers often scrambled to provide adequate care for their children when working outside the home. If they were able, they advertised for other women to assist with their domestic duties, such as cleaning their homes or watching their children. Some mothers relied on extended family, neighbors, or an older daughter to help with childcare while they worked. Whether they were following the call to aid in the war effort or working to support their families, mothers frequently struggled to balance their many responsibilities. Yet, in America's time of need, mothers did what mothers do best: They selflessly devoted themselves to those who depended on them.

Janet "Jessie" Woodrow Wilson

Mother of Woodrow Wilson

Janet "Jessie" Woodrow Wilson was born in 1826 in Carlisle, England, the daughter of Reverend Dr. Thomas Woodrow and Marion Williamson of Scotland. She came with her parents to America in 1836 and settled in the South, where she eventually married Reverend Joseph Ruggles Wilson, a Presbyterian minister, and gave birth to Woodrow Wilson in Staunton, Virginia, in 1856. During the Civil War, Wilson's father was a chaplain in the Confederate army, and his mother helped set up a hospital at their church in Augusta, Georgia. Wilson's mother doted on her son and the two had such a close relationship that, remembering her to his wife, Wilson recalled: "I remember how I clung to her (a laughed-at 'mamma's boy') till I was a great big fellow: but love of the best womanhood came to me and entered my heart through those apron-strings." It is fitting that President Wilson, so enamored of his mother, established Mother's Day in 1914, so that all Americans could celebrate their mothers as he celebrated and honored his.

"I seem to feel still the touch of her hand, and the sweet, steadying influence of her wonderful character. I thank God to have had such a mother!"

—President Woodrow Wilson

MOTHERS AND SONS

There's an old folk saying that men marry women who remind them of their mothers. While this may or may not be true, few relationships are so highly revered as those between mothers and their sons. While sometimes this bond is portrayed in popular culture as a little too close (think Ray Romano and interfering Doris Roberts on *Everybody Loves Raymond*—or, of course, Norman Bates and "Mother" in *Psycho*), the fact is that mothers have inspired many of our country's leaders, from Woodrow Wilson; to Calvin Coolidge, who died carrying a picture of his mother, Victoria, in his watch case; to Vietnam-era president Lyndon B. Johnson, who referred to his mother, Rebekah, as "the greatest female I have ever known, without any exceptions."

MOTHER'S DAY 1918

"Sons are the anchors of a mother's life."

—*Sophocles*

When we think of mothers and sons, words like *love*, *loyalty*, and *devotion* come to mind. And yet, there is always a tinge of the bittersweet—whether the little boy Mom has held so dearly goes on to be a soldier on the front lines, the president of the United States, or simply a grown man with his own spouse and children that fill his heart. Perhaps that is why the mothers of television and movies are alternately portrayed as meddlers and saints. Because when it comes to raising sons, motherhood is ultimately about giving your all—and then doing your best to let go.

OPPOSITE, LEFT Acclaimed cartoonist Clifford K. Berryman envisions a soldier writing to and thinking of his mother on Mother's Day 1918. **LEFT** Rebekah Johnson, mother of President Lyndon B. Johnson, with her son, at a 1941 senatorial campaign rally. **ABOVE** Still of Ray Romano and Doris Roberts from *Everybody Loves Raymond*.

FOUR

Betty Dons Her Apron

THE ROARING TWENTIES

"A hundred men may make an encampment.
It takes a woman to make a home."

—CHINESE PROVERB

IN THE YEARS following World War I, women enjoyed more freedoms—both socially and politically. The number of women who worked outside the home continued to rise in the 1920s, although only a small percentage of those workers included married women and mothers. The nation's total wealth more than doubled between 1920 and 1929, creating a "consumer society" that led to many ads directly targeting Mom. Betty Crocker® was created in 1921 (see page 46), and quickly became an American icon of the home and kitchen.

Technology was also changing day-to-day life for mothers as advances in modern machinery, such as vacuum cleaners, electric floor polishers, and home refrigerators, eased their domestic burdens.

OPPOSITE Detail of an ad from 1929 for General Electric in the *Saturday Evening Post*; the relatively new invention of the electric refrigerator helped moms keep their children's food safe to eat.

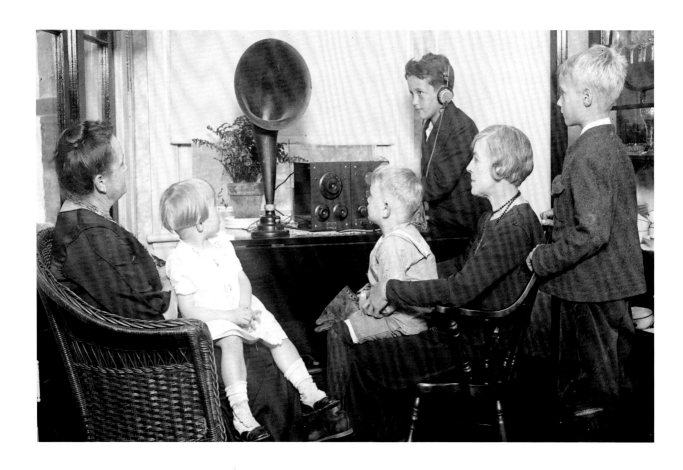

The way families experienced entertainment was also changing with the growing popularity of radio and film. And with the rise of the Harlem Renaissance in New York, African American women and mothers were adding their voices and experiences to the nation's literary and arts scene.

And, of course, in politics, women across the United States finally enjoyed the right to vote, after the ratification of the Nineteenth Amendment in 1920. In what came down to a harrowing vote in Tennessee's state legislature, twenty-four-year-old Harry Burn changed his position and voted for the measure—leading Tennessee to become the required thirty-sixth state to ratify the amendment and pave the way for its adoption. What changed young Burn's mind? Perhaps it had something to do with a note he received from his mother, Phoebe Ensminger Burn, who wrote to her son, "Hurrah, and vote for suffrage!" and urged him to "be a good boy" and help the cause. Burn later acknowledged the influence of his mother, stating, "I know that a mother's advice is always safest for her boy to follow, and my mother wanted me to vote for ratification."

Food for Thought

Flappers may have captured the popular imagination in the 1920s, but America's advertisers were confident that Mom still controlled the kitchen. Ads stressing conservation and war rationing gave way to images that were more carefree and fun, and that appealed to a consumer society with money to spend. According to *Ad Age*, by 1925, almost 40 percent of the US workforce

> "The right of citizens of the United States to vote shall not be denied or abridged by the United States or by any State on account of sex."
>
> —Nineteenth Amendment, ratified on August 18, 1920

earned $2,000 or more a year (equivalent to about $30,000 today). While men were the primary wage earners, middle-class women were making buying decisions about their kitchens and homes, and they now had more disposable income and—with modern machinery—more time with which to do so.

Ads in magazines such as the *Ladies' Home Journal* and *Good Housekeeping* peddled everything from toothpaste and kitchen appliances to makeup and antiaging creams. Food advertisements targeting mothers were especially popular in the 1920s, from companies such as General Mills®, Campbell's®, Heinz®, and more. Mothers in ads were often seen joyfully serving meals and snacks to children, with an emphasis on keeping their kids healthy. Other advertisers promised to reduce Mom's workload and turn her kitchen into a den of modernity. The young, liberated flapper was seen as the modern ideal of the time. While mothers might not be able to party like flappers, they could create their own version of freedom by using modern cooking methods and spending less time cleaning clothes and buying groceries. Without these pesky household burdens, they could focus more on being doting mothers and attentive wives.

Just in case mothers weren't getting the message, advertisers invented fictional spokespeople to help them run their kitchens: Betty Crocker promoted Gold Medal® flour and Mary Hale Martin signed advice columns and replied to customer letters for Libby's® foods. From print ads to radio, advertisers were sparing little expense in courting the American mom.

"*Look, Mother. I can polish too!*"

IT is easy NOW to have beautiful waxed floors in every room. It makes no difference whether the floors are old or new—of wood, linoleum, tile or composition. And it matters not how the floors are now finished.
You can easily give the linoleum and all the floors in your home a deep, lustrous, lasting brilliance, by polishing them with Johnson's Liquid Wax.
Johnson Waxed floors, besides being beautiful, have many advantages. They are not slippery, do not collect dust—"traffic spots" in doorways can be rewaxed in a few seconds without going over the entire floor.
Johnson's Liquid Wax cleans, polishes, preserves and protects in one operation. No matter how worn, you will be surprised and delighted by the remarkable change that Johnson's Polishing Wax can effect in their appearance.
Johnson's Polishing Wax is very economical, a little Wax goes a long way, and the brilliant finish it gives is most durable, making polishing less frequent.

In all Sizes from all Dealers
1/-, 2/6, 4/-, 7/6, 14/- & 24/6

JOHNSON'S WAX
Electric Floor Polisher

If you prefer to polish your floors electrically, HIRE this new labour-saving machine from your local dealer to Wax-polish all your floors. Ten times faster than other methods. It works from any lamp socket for less than 1d. an hour. Eliminates stooping, kneeling and all messy rags and pails. Make arrangements now to HIRE a JOHNSON'S Wax Electric Floor Polisher for a few hours at the rate of 5/- a day, or 3/- a half-day.

If your Dealer cannot supply you, write us for the name of a Dealer who can

To purchase a Johnson's Wax Electric Floor Polisher outright means an investment of only £9 . 18 . 6.

S. C. JOHNSON & SON LTD., WEST DRAYTON
MIDDLESEX
"*The Floor Finishing Authorities*"

JOHNSON'S POLISHING WAX
PASTE *or* LIQUID ~ CLEANS, POLISHES, PRESERVES ALL FLOORS

LEFT 1920s technology helped busy moms keep house in many new ways, such as with this electric Johnson's Wax® floor polisher. **RIGHT** A hot chocolate ad from the 1920s.

BLUE LABEL FOODS

BLUE LABEL
TRADE MARK

CHOCOLATTA
TRADE MARK

A FOOD BEVERAGE

SCIENTIFICALLY PREPARED FROM
PURE CHOCOLATE, SUGAR
AND POWDERED SKIMMED MILK

NOURISHING · STIMULATING
DIGESTIBLE

CURTICE BROTHERS CO.,
ROCHESTER, N.Y.

William van Dresser

Perfect Hot Chocolate

—can be made from Chocolatta by adding boiling water only.

Chocolatta is a scientifically prepared chocolate beverage in powdered form—perfectly blended chocolate, sugar and milk.

These three foods are nourishing and wholesome. In the preparation of Chocolatta the fat globules in the chocolate are so broken up that Chocolatta is easily digested.

Chocolatta is easily and quickly prepared in the cup by simply adding boiling water—no material wasted, and only the cup and spoon to wash.

You can depend on the absolute purity and delicious goodness of every Blue Label Food—Soups, Chili Sauce, Ketchup, Canned Fruits and Vegetables, Boned Turkey and Chicken, Jams, Jellies and Preserves—ready for your instant use.

From soup to sweets you can serve a complete and perfect meal of Blue Label Foods.

*Write for our booklet "Pictorial History of Hospitality."
It contains many good menus and recipes. We shall be
pleased to send it if you will mention your grocer's name.*

Phoebe Dickerson Harding

Mother of Warren G. Harding

Phoebe Dickerson Harding (1843–1910) was a farm girl from central Ohio who fell in love with her neighbor, George Tyron Harding II. The two married in secret, with Phoebe's sister as a witness, before her new husband left to enlist in the Union army. Phoebe Harding went on to have eight children—six of them lived to adulthood and two died as young children. She was devoted to her eldest child, Warren, making time to read to him each day and placing an emphasis on education. After the war, her husband became a physician. Already a midwife who delivered babies for local mothers, Phoebe Harding studied and eventually became a doctor as well, an unusual distinction for a woman. She died at age sixty-six, eleven years before her son, the twenty-ninth US president (1921–23), entered the White House.

"I can never forget the love and devotion for his mother . . . his regular visits with an offering of flowers, his implicit confidence in her and his admiration of her."

—Abigail Victoria Harding, Warren G. Harding's sister, to Reverend William J. Hampton, 1921

"Every Woman's Life Is a Soap Opera."

—Title of an Irna Phillips article in McCall's, March 1965

Around the Radio

On November 2, 1920, radio station KDKA in Pittsburgh made the nation's first commercial broadcast, airing the results of the election between Warren G. Harding and James Cox. While radio—invented in the late nineteenth century—wasn't new, it was still in its infancy. Primitive radio transmissions were used for military communication during World War I, and afterward, radio was largely the terrain of technical-minded hobbyists. But both technology and available programming grew quickly. Between 1923 and 1930, 60 percent of American families purchased radios. By the end of the 1920s, there were radios in more than twelve million households, according to James Ciment's *Encyclopedia of the Jazz Age*.

Families gathered around radios to hear news and listen to everything from jazz to Sunday sermons. With radio, advertisers had a new medium for reaching mothers. Companies such as A&P and Ipana Toothpaste Company sponsored shows with musical numbers to capture listeners' attention. But it was in the 1930s, with the advent of soap operas—the "soap" referring to the shows' sponsors, mostly manufacturers of household cleaning products—that radio advertising to the American mom came of age. The first soap opera, *Painted Dreams*, aired in 1930 and followed conversations between Mother Moynihan and her unmarried daughter. Played by series creator and writer Irna Phillips, considered by many to be the "Queen of the Soaps," Mother Moynihan's character was a wise and kindly widow who offered a traditional view of motherhood as a woman's path to true happiness, while her daughter was more modern with career ambitions. Despite their commercial origins, radio "soaps" were often written by women, and featured storylines and issues important to housewives and mothers of the time.

OPPOSITE Phoebe Dickerson Harding as a young woman, c. 1868.
ABOVE Irna Phillips working, c. 1940.

FUN FACT Irna Phillips (1901–73) went on to create some of America's most beloved and long-running soap operas, including *Guiding Light*, *As the World Turns*, and *Another World*. She was also a single mother, adopting two children later in her life.

The Birth of Betty Crocker

The story of Betty Crocker—known as "The First Lady of Food"—began almost a hundred years ago. In 1921, the Washburn Crosby Company—the Minneapolis flour-milling company that was a predecessor of General Mills, Inc.—ran a promotion for Gold Medal flour in the *Saturday Evening Post*, challenging readers to send in a completed jigsaw puzzle in order to receive a small prize. The company received thousands of responses, along with questions from readers about baking. In responding to readers' letters, the company created a fictional character with the first name "Betty" and the last name of a retired company director, William G. Crocker. And just like that, an icon was born.

The Washburn Crosby Company went on to sponsor cooking schools and a Home Service Department staffed with home economists, which eventually led to the formation of the Betty Crocker Kitchens. In 1924, Betty Crocker made her debut on daytime radio's first cooking show, *The Betty Crocker Cooking School of the Air*, broadcast in Minneapolis. By 1927, the program went national, airing on NBC radio. Betty Crocker owed much of her success to Marjorie Child Husted, the business-woman and home economist who headed the Betty Crocker Homemaking Service, served as the icon's voice on the radio, and edited *Betty Crocker's Picture Cookbook*. Betty was later played by actress Adelaide Hawley on television in the 1950s and was represented by various other actresses.

Betty's popularity continued to grow. According to *Fortune* magazine, in April 1945, Betty Crocker was the second best-known woman in America, right after First Lady Eleanor Roosevelt.

While many people today are familiar with Betty Crocker recipes, cook-books, and products, they may be less aware of another important role the brand's spokesperson played in American history. During World War II, in 1945, Betty Crocker broadcast *Our Nation's Rations*—a radio program produced by General Mills at the request of the US Office of War Information—advising women on how to feed their families with rationed food supplies. Adding to Betty Crocker's patriotic endeavors, almost seven million copies of "Your Share," a wartime recipe pamphlet published under her name, were distributed at this time.

FUN FACT During Betty Crocker's four-month radio program, the fictional icon provided American homemakers with information about war bonds, Red Cross efforts, and food rationing. The legendary homemaker also interviewed soldiers, government officials, and other experts on how to contribute on the home front.

EDUCATION NUMBER

The CRISIS

Vol. 20 No. 3   JULY, 1920   Whole No. 117

ABOVE Cover of the *Crisis*, July 1920, edited by Jessie Redmon Fauset. **RIGHT** Jessie Redmon Fauset photograph, c. 1918. **OPPOSITE** Title page of *Bronze*, 1922, by Georgia Douglas Johnson, with an engraving of her portrait.

Women of the Harlem Renaissance

During World War I, increased industrialization and economic opportunities led many African Americans to leave the rural South and resettle in Northern cities—the beginning of what would be called the Great Migration. New York City's Harlem became a focal point for African American culture of the time, witnessing an explosion of blues and jazz music; new styles of poetry, fiction, and theater; and publications including the *Crisis*, the magazine of the National Association for the Advancement of Colored People (NAACP), founded in 1910. Founding editor W. E. B. Du Bois initially intended for the magazine to "set forth those facts and arguments which show the danger of race prejudice," as he wrote in the first issue. However, during the early 1920s, the magazine became a showcase for the rising cultural movement, under the direction of writer and educator Jessie Redmon Fauset.

Georgia Douglas Johnson

(c. 1880–1966)

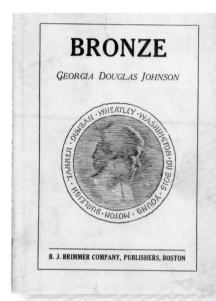

BRONZE

GEORGIA DOUGLAS JOHNSON

·DUNBAR· WHEATLEY ·WASHINGTON· DU BOIS· YOUNG· BURLEIGH· TANNER· MOTON·

B. J. BRIMMER COMPANY, PUBLISHERS, BOSTON

Georgia Douglas Johnson, one of the most famous poets of the Harlem Renaissance, was born in Atlanta, Georgia. She graduated from Atlanta University Normal School (teaching college) in 1896 and studied music at Oberlin Conservatory, before becoming an assistant principal in Atlanta. She then moved with her husband, ambitious politician Henry Lincoln Johnson, to Washington, DC.

Despite her husband's expectations that she follow a traditional role of wife and mother to their two sons, she pursued her artistic ambitions, publishing three of her poems in the *Crisis* in 1916, and going on to publish four books of poetry: *The Heart of a Woman* (1918), *Bronze* (1922), *An Autumn Love Cycle* (1928), and *Share My World* (1962). The Saturday night salons she hosted at her home are now legendary, attended by such luminaries as Langston Hughes, Jean Toomer, Zora Neale Hurston, Alain Locke, Jessie Redmon Fauset, and more.

In 1925, Douglas Johnson's husband died, leaving her to raise her two teenage sons on her own. She worked tirelessly and managed to put both of her sons through college. Never giving up on her artistic ambitions, she also wrote a number of plays and a weekly syndicated newspaper column, "Homely Philosophy." She died in 1966, leaving a legacy as a nurturer of talent and one of the most important voices of the Harlem Renaissance.

"The heart of a woman goes forth with the dawn,
As a lone bird, soft winging, so restlessly on."

—*Georgia Douglas Johnson, "The Heart of a Woman," 1918*

As literary editor of the *Crisis* from 1919 to 1926, and editor of NAACP's short-lived children's magazine, the *Brownies' Book*, Fauset discovered and encouraged some of the most famous poets and writers of the period.

Today, the best-known writers of the Harlem Renaissance tend to be men: Langston Hughes, Claude McKay, Countee Cullen. However, women writers and poets also shaped the cultural movement, writing about the experiences of the African American woman, from artistry and struggle to politics and motherhood. In addition to Jessie Redmon Fauset, influential women of the Harlem Renaissance included Gwendolyn Bennett, Zora Neale Hurston, Georgia Douglas Johnson, and others. From her home in Washington, DC, poet and playwright Georgia Douglas Johnson, widowed mother of two sons, ran one of the most famous literary salons of the Harlem Renaissance (see previous page).

The topic of motherhood wasn't just the domain of female writers, however. Two of Langston Hughes's most powerful poems—"Mother to Son" and "The Negro Mother"— recount the historical struggle of the African American mother and continue to move and inspire readers today.

ABOVE Portrait of Zora Neale Hurston, 1938. **TOP RIGHT** Illustration by Gwendolyn Bennett on the cover of the *Opportunity* journal, July 1926. **RIGHT** Cover of the NAACP's *Brownies' Book* magazine from January 1920.

Mom at the Movies— Classic Cinema

While the technology to create moving pictures dates back to the late 1800s, it took several decades for film to develop into an industry resembling the one we know today. Films were silent until the 1927 release of *The Jazz Singer*, which added a synchronized audio track and launched the rise of "talkies." During the mid-1910s, the "nickelodeons" of the early twentieth century—which showed short films for a nickel—began to be replaced by larger cinemas; at the same time, the motion picture industry began its western exodus from Fort Lee, New Jersey, to Hollywood. By the 1920s, more than eight hundred feature films were being released a year—the industry's greatest output in US history—starring recognizable actors such as Charlie Chaplin and Mary Pickford. Americans had a new, mature form of entertainment, and American moms had new onscreen counterparts.

ABOVE A still of Mary Pickford in the 1921 silent film version of *Little Lord Fauntleroy*; she played the roles of both Cedric Errol and the Widow Errol.

While early films focused on swashbucklers, Westerns, romances, comedies, and gangster films, Mom wasn't left out. Dolores Costello, once known as "The Goddess of the Silent Screen" (she is best known today as the grandmother of Drew Barrymore), charmed audiences as the selfless mother in the 1936 drama *Little Lord Fauntleroy*, based on the 1886 novel by Frances Hodgson Burnett. In the movie, Costello's character, a widow called "Dearest" by her son, sacrifices her own happiness so that her son Cedric ("Ceddie") can live with his English grandfather, the Earl of Dorincourt, who had disowned her husband for marrying her. In the end, she is rewarded for being such a devoted mother and is brought to live with Cedric on the earl's estate.

Indeed, the sacrificial mother seems to be a theme in early cinema. The 1937 film *Stella Dallas*—remade from the 1925 silent film, which was also produced by Samuel Goldwyn—starred Barbara Stanwyck in the title role, for which she was nominated for an Academy Award for Best Actress in a Leading Role. In the film, social climber Stella realizes she can only give her beloved daughter, Laurel, the life she deserves by letting her go. Stella selflessly sends Laurel to live with her wealthy father and stepmother, allowing Laurel

to escape Stella's working-class roots and find love and happiness in high society. Similarly, in the 1945 film noir *Mildred Pierce*, the title character, played by Joan Crawford, devotes her life to trying to make her unappreciative daughter happy. Her husband leaves her for caring more about her children than him, and from there the sacrifices continue, as Mildred enters into a loveless marriage to improve her daughter's station.

ABOVE A poster for *Little Lord Fauntleroy*, starring Dolores Costello and Freddie Batholomew, 1936. **OPPOSITE, LEFT** Poster for *Stella Dallas*, 1937, with Barbara Stanwyck as the selfless mother, Stella Martin, and John Boles as her husband, Stephen Dallas; their daughter, Laurel, was played by Anne Shirley as a young woman. **OPPOSITE, RIGHT** Still of Greer Garson, Walter Pidgeon, and their onscreen children in the Oscar-winning *Mrs. Miniver*, 1942.

The woman you will never forget...

VULGAR, TAWDRY, MAGNIFICENT

SAMUEL GOLDWYN
presents

STELLA DALLAS

WITH

As always, mothers were also valuable in war propaganda. In 1942's *Mrs. Miniver*, which won the Academy Award for Best Picture, Greer Garson depicted a British mother who courageously holds her family together during the height of Nazi aggression in England. While classic cinema offered films for all tastes, moviegoers could always sympathize with the devoted, selfless mothers of the silver screen.

"The big world may be better because my little child was born. And that is best of all, Ceddie—it is better than everything else, that the world should be a little better because a man has lived— even ever so little better, dearest."
—*Frances Hodgson Burnett, Little Lord Fauntleroy, 1886*

FIVE

Lean Times

THE GREAT DEPRESSION

"A mother is one to whom you hurry when you are troubled."
—EMILY DICKINSON

T HE GREAT DEPRESSION brought difficulties to many American families. In many ways, mothers' roles were more important than ever: With their husbands taking pay cuts or losing their jobs, reducing household expenses and finding ways to do more with less became pivotal. Many middle-class women had to work outside the home to provide needed income; for poor women or women of color, this wasn't always a change. Families in the Plains states were hit especially hard, as droughts and dust storms forced many into poverty.

To distract themselves from economic realities, families continued to gather around the radio and went to sporting events and the cinema. Advertisers, struggling to sway Americans during tough financial times, encouraged women to "buy American"— especially when it came to clothing, as the US fashion industry strengthened.

OPPOSITE A contemporary colorized version of *Migrant Mother*, Dorothea Lange's iconic 1936 photograph (see pages 61–63), which epitomizes the struggles, especially of mothers, during the Great Depression.

MORE SECURITY FOR THE AMERICAN FAMILY

WHEN AN INSURED WORKER DIES, LEAVING DEPENDENT CHILDREN AND A WIDOW, BOTH MOTHER AND CHILDREN RECEIVE MONTHLY BENEFITS UNTIL THE LATTER REACH 18.

ABOVE This US government poster, aimed at mothers, promoted the Social Security Act, c. 1935.
OPPOSITE WPA "Nurse the Baby" poster by graphic artist Erik Hans Krause, c. 1937; the Roosevelt administration was an early advocate for nursing.

Other advertisers pushed the economy and time-saving aspects of their products, understanding that, in the midst of economic turmoil, American mothers were doing more and struggling to help their families get by.

A Message from the Government

America's Great Depression began after the Stock Market Crash of 1929 and lasted for a decade after that. As consumer spending dropped and fewer people invested their money, Americans faced rampant unemployment, pay cuts, and food shortages. The Great Depression reached its peak in 1933, with fifteen million Americans unemployed. While many men were left without work, for mothers, familiar challenges intensified: they had to feed their families with smaller budgets, keep house using less electricity, and perform tasks they may have previously paid others to do. As Eleanor Roosevelt stated, in her 1933 book *It's Up to the Women*, "Practically every woman, whether she is rich or poor, is facing today a reduction of income."

In 1932, Americans elected Franklin Delano Roosevelt as their thirty-second president. After entering office in March 1933, FDR brought many changes, including the 1935 Social Security Act, which focused on providing aid for older Americans, children, the unemployed, and others. To gain public support for these programs, as in times past, the government issued posters aimed at mothers. One poster, depicting a loving mother with a smiling baby, promised "More Security for the American Family." Other posters appealed to widows or promoted the Aid to Dependent Children program. But the government wasn't only interested in struggling families' economic security. One poster from the Federal Art Project, sponsored by the Works Progress Administration, encouraged mothers to "Nurse the Baby," advising it was "Your Protection Against Trouble"—publicly promoting breastfeeding as early as the 1930s.

NURSE THE BABY
YOUR PROTECTION AGAINST TROUBLE

WPA FEDERAL ART PROJECT

"Women, whether subtly or vociferously, have always been a tremendous power in the destiny of the world."

—Eleanor Roosevelt, It's Up to the Women, *1933*

Ma Joad, *The Grapes of Wrath*

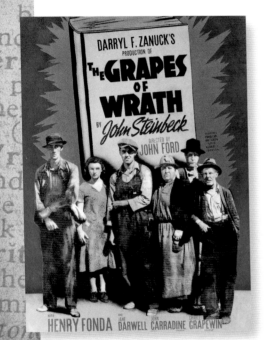

There may, perhaps, be no better model of a tough Depression-era mother holding her impoverished family together than Ma Joad of John Steinbeck's 1939 classic, *The Grapes of Wrath*. In this harrowing tale, Ma Joad and her family of tenant farmers leave Dust Bowl–afflicted Oklahoma to find fruit-picking work in the promised land of California. Facing sickness, hunger, and a constant struggle to stay together, the Joad family endures one obstacle after another in an attempt to earn a decent wage and survive. Through it all, Ma Joad remains strong and does whatever needs to be done, from burning her possessions when the family truck is overloaded, to taking care of Grampa and, after he dies of a stroke, preparing his dead body for burial, to buying groceries and turning the family's slim earnings into a meal. Whether or not they were farmers or even dealing with unemployment, readers all over the United States could relate to Ma Joad's steady determination to guide and protect her family in impossible circumstances.

"She seemed to know, to accept, to welcome
her position, the citadel of the family,
the strong place that could not be taken."

—*John Steinbeck*, The Grapes of Wrath, *1939*

OPPOSITE Poster for the 1940 Daryl Zanuck version of Steinbeck's *The Grapes of Wrath*, starring Jane Darwell as the indomitable Ma Joad and Henry Fonda as her son Tom.
LEFT Dorothea Lange posing in California with her camera, 1936.

Through Her Lens

It was one thing for Americans to hear or read about the plight of farmers and migrant laborers. But nothing brought their difficult conditions to light like the images captured by photographer Dorothea Lange. Her work for the Farm Security Administration during the Great Depression humanized the suffering of families, helped bring aid to those in need, and contributed to the development of modern documentary photography.

A survivor of childhood polio who walked with a permanent limp, Lange, who was born in 1895 in Hoboken, New Jersey, studied photography at Columbia University in New York before moving to San Francisco and settling in Berkeley. In 1920, she married painter Maynard Dixon and the couple had two sons.

> **BY THE NUMBERS** In 1935–36, the median family income was $1,160, meaning families had roughly $20–$25 a week to pay for the things they needed, according to the Gilder Lehrman Institute of American History.

FIRST AID
NURSERY

It was during the Great Depression that Lange found her calling, as she photographed the jobless on the streets and at soup kitchens. Her work led to her employment with the Resettlement Agency (RA), later known as the Farm Security Administration (FSA). This agency, part of FDR's New Deal, relocated families, especially those fleeing the droughts of the Great Plains, to relief camps in California.

The RA wasn't initially a popular program, and the government sought ways to gain public support. In 1935,

RA chief Rexford Tugwell appointed Roy Stryker as the head of a historical section to document the suffering of Americans and the benefits that RA programs provided to destitute farmers. Through an assemblage of talented photographers including Lange, Walker Evans, Arthur Rothstein, and more, Stryker and the Historical Section created a pictorial archive of the Great Depression's impact on rural America. The photographs reached the masses through popular magazines of the time, such as *Life*, *Look*, and *Fortune*.

In 1935, Lange divorced her husband and married Paul Schuster Taylor, an economics professor. Together the couple documented rural poverty and the life of sharecroppers, migrant workers, and displaced farm families. During this time, Lange took one of the most iconic photographs of the Depression, *Migrant Mother* (1936)

(see colorized version, page 54, and pages 62–63), which captured a desperate mother with her two children. The government subsequently sent twenty thousand pounds of food to the camp. John Steinbeck featured Lange's photographs in his *The Harvest Gypsies*, a series of articles he wrote for the *San Francisco News* about migrant workers in the Salinas Valley.

Dorothea Lange died in 1965. In 2008, she was inducted into the California Hall of Fame.

OPPOSITE A Lange photograph of a nursery school for children of migrant workers, near Bakersfield, California, 1936. ABOVE LEFT A migrant cotton picker and her baby were captured by Lange's lens in Maricopa County, Arizona, 1940. ABOVE RIGHT A homeless mother and the youngest of her seven children pose for Lange on a highway near Brawley, California, 1939.

RIGHT An FSA log sheet, with a photograph of *Migrant Mother* in the center, indicating the publications where Lange's influential picture appeared from 1936 to 1940, including the *New York Times* (twice) and the *Washington Post*.
OPPOSITE An outtake from Lange's 1936 photo session with Florence Owens Thompson—the "Migrant Mother"—and her children.

MIGRANT MOTHER AND CHILDREN
CALIFORNIA

PHOTO BY LANGE

PUBLICATIONS WHICH THEY HAVE APPEARED
1935 -'36 -'37 -'38 -'39

PAPER	DATE	PAPER	DATE
New York Times	July 5, 1936		
San Francisco News	3-11-36		
"	Oct. 5, 1936		
U. S. News	1936		
San Francisco Chronicle	3-7-36		
Theater And Film	April, 1936		
Scholastic	Sept. 26, 1936		
Survey Graphic	Sept. 1936		
Building America	1937		
Midweek Pictorial	Oct. 17, 1936		
Svetozor	1937		
Survey Graphic	1936		
Washington Post	June 23, 1938		
Epworth Highroad	Feb. 1938		
Washington Post	March 7, 1937		
New York Times	July 5, 1935		
San Francisco Examiner	Feb 5, 1936		
Social Action	Feb 1937		
Sunday Photograph - Bri...	June 9, 1940		
The Epworth Highroad	July, 1940		

Who Was the "Migrant Mother"?

Florence Owens Thompson was born Florence Leona Christie in 1903 in Indian Territory in what is now Oklahoma. Married at age seventeen, by 1931 she had given birth to six children, and her husband died of tuberculosis. She ultimately had four more children, three with boyfriend Jim Hill, and worked various jobs to support her family.

One day in March 1936, she and Hill had been driving with the children, looking for work, when their car broke down near Nipomo in California. They pulled into a migrant camp where pea pickers were left without work after a frost. When Lange approached the thirty-two-year-old mother, she and her children were waiting while Hill and her older sons went to get parts for the car. Lange took a series of photos, which were later published in the *San Francisco News*. The migrant mother continued to work, eventually marrying hospital administrator George Thompson after World War II.

Thompson was identified as the "migrant mother" in 1978 by a *Modesto Bee* reporter. In 1983, when she was suffering from cancer, her family received tens of thousands of dollars in donations. Later that year, she died surrounded by family.

> "A Legend of the Strength of American Motherhood."
> —*Epitaph on the gravestone of Florence Owens Thompson*

First Lady
Eleanor Roosevelt

The longest-serving First Lady of the United States, Anna Eleanor Roosevelt (1884–1962) is today considered an American icon, remembered for her humanitarian work and advocacy of women's rights. Married to Franklin Delano Roosevelt, Eleanor held the title of First Lady from 1933 until 1945, occupying the White House during the Depression and World War II.

The niece of President Theodore Roosevelt, Eleanor was born into a high-society family in Manhattan. Despite her family's wealth, she had a difficult childhood, losing her parents and brother at a young age. She attended school in England, where she was influenced by noted feminist headmistress Marie Souvestre. After Eleanor returned to the United States, she attracted the attention of her distant cousin, Franklin Delano, and the two became engaged in 1903, despite his mother's objections. The couple married in 1905 and went on to have six children: Anna, James, Franklin, Elliott, Franklin Delano Jr., and John.

When her husband developed polio in 1921, Eleanor encouraged him to remain in politics and began making public appearances on his behalf. She raised funds for the Women's Trade Union League, which advocated for causes including the abolition of child labor. When Franklin Delano became governor of New York, Eleanor traveled the state making speeches and other public appearances.

OPPOSITE Eleanor Roosevelt, c. 1945. **ABOVE** Eleanor Roosevelt, President Franklin D. Roosevelt, and their son, Franklin D. Roosevelt Jr., at the 1933 presidential inauguration.

"I think, at a child's birth, if a mother could ask a fairy godmother to endow it with the most useful gift, that gift should be curiosity."

—*Eleanor Roosevelt*

As First Lady of the United States, Eleanor Roosevelt broadened the role, giving regular press conferences, writing newspaper columns, and hosting a radio show—all firsts for a First Lady. She championed many causes, including civil rights and women's inclusion in New Deal initiatives, focusing on the plight of unemployed women.

During World War II, she encouraged women to enter the military and work in defense industries, actively supporting legislation to create subsidized daycare centers for mothers working in these roles (see pages 70–71). When these childcare centers closed after the war, Eleanor continued to advocate for their necessity, writing in her "My Day" newspaper column in September 1945: "But we have to face the fact that there are married women with young children who have to go to work. In such cases, it would seem to be in the interests of the community to organize childcare centers and see that they are properly run."

After her husband's death in 1945, Eleanor remained politically active and was appointed by President Truman as a delegate to the United Nations General Assembly and chairperson of the UN Commission on Human Rights. She remained an advocate for humanitarian causes throughout her life. She died in 1962 at the age of seventy-eight.

OPPOSITE Roosevelt greets female enlistees at Sampson Air Force Base in Geneva, New York, 1943. **TOP** Roosevelt and President Harry S. Truman display a UN flag, Washington, DC, 1950. **BOTTOM** Eleanor Roosevelt surrounded by children, c. 1935; Roosevelt was a passionate advocate for subsidized daycare centers for working mothers.

SIX

We Can Do It!

WORLD WAR II

*"My experience has been that work is almost the best way
to pull oneself out of the depths."*

—ELEANOR ROOSEVELT

ON DECEMBER 7, 1941, the unthinkable happened. The Japanese military bombed the US naval base at Pearl Harbor, and Americans found themselves preparing for another war overseas. World War II brought many mothers out of the home and into the factory, where they were needed to support the war effort in addition to filling other jobs vacated by men, serving as office workers, drivers, steel mill workers, and more. Government propaganda posters and general sentiment portrayed this work as patriotic, with Rosie the Riveter images encouraging women to do their part. However, for women with children, the demands were often difficult. To meet their needs, daycare centers became common, offering a solution for mothers who wanted or needed to earn income for their families and contribute to the war effort. For many moms, daycare allowed for postwar employment as well, starting a trend that continues today.

OPPOSITE A real-life Rosie the Riveter operates a hand drill while working on an A-31 Vengeance dive bomber at a Vultee Aircraft plant in Nashville, Tennessee, 1943.

Bye-Bye, Baby

In the 1940s, America's children had a new uncle in their corner: Uncle Sam. With America's munitions factories and other industries filled with hardworking Rosie the Riveters aiding in war production, a question quickly arose: Who would care for America's children?

Enter the US government and the Community Facilities Act of 1940, or Lanham Act, which subsidized daycare centers across America during the war. Between 1943 and 1946, the government granted $52 million for childcare under this act to communities that could demonstrate a war-related need for this service. Indeed, with so many women entering the workforce, many mothers were in desperate need of help. According to the Library of Congress, nineteen million women were in the workforce in July 1944, compared to thirteen million in 1940. And while it's not certain how many mothers worked during this time, participation of married women in the workforce grew from 15 percent in 1940 to 23 percent in 1944. That's a lot of women seeking work/life balance.

Even with the help of the government, life wasn't easy for the working mothers and wives of World War II. When they returned home from long days cleaning bombers, building planes, or working in offices, they had housework to contend with and children who needed them. There was also a significant pay gap, with women earning around 50 percent of what men did for the same work. But at the very least, the subsidized care provided mothers with some peace of mind that their children were in good, affordable hands.

After the war, the grants ended and the government daycare centers closed. Women were expected to return home when their husbands came back from service, to make room in the workplace for returning soldiers. Yet, women's employment continued to rise after the war, as women sought to continue working for reasons other than patriotic duty. Despite cultural norms about a woman's place, a tide had turned in the roles of women and mothers.

Moms Go to Work

In 1942, President Roosevelt created the Office of War Information (OWI), which sold the war through Hollywood movie studios, the ever-growing radio market, and, of course, good old propaganda posters. Gangsters were replaced by Nazis and Japanese as villains in wartime films. Families listened to Roosevelt's "Fireside Chats" on the radio. And posters at schools,

BY THE NUMBERS
According to the Congressional Research Service, in July 1944, there were more than 3,000 federally subsidized childcare centers in the United States, serving more than 130,000 children. Childcare cost parents around fifty cents per child per day, raised to seventy-five cents in July 1945—in today's money, that's around ten dollars a day!

Sara Roosevelt

Mother of Franklin Delano Roosevelt

While her son led America through the Depression and World War II, inspiring the masses with quotes such as "The only thing we have to fear is fear itself," Sara Ann Delano Roosevelt was a commanding woman in her own right. Born in Newburgh, New York, in 1854, she was the daughter of a merchant who grew rich in the tea and opium trade in China, and she spent part of her childhood in Hong Kong. At age twenty-six, she married widower James Roosevelt, and gave birth to her only child, Franklin, in 1882.

Mother and son were close during FDR's childhood, as she lavished attention on him. When Sara's husband died in 1900, she continued to focus her energies on her son. She followed him to Boston, moving to an apartment there while he was at Harvard. When he fell in love with Eleanor and wanted to propose, she tried to stop him; when she was unsuccessful, she convinced him to keep the engagement secret for a year. After her son's marriage, Sara had built a double townhouse in Manhattan—one for Franklin and Eleanor and one for herself, with a connecting door between the two. Despite a supposedly tense relationship with her daughter-in-law, she was actively involved in her son's and grandchildren's lives. She was the first presidential mom to be able to vote for her son (three times) and authored a memoir, *My Boy Franklin* (1933). She died in 1941.

"I think of you night and day."

—Sara Roosevelt to Franklin Delano Roosevelt, 1941

stores, and other public places were filled with images of "Mothers of Men" supporting the Red Cross's wartime efforts, buying war bonds, and performing their patriotic duties at wartime-production factories.

There was a great need for war production during World War II, and, despite initial resistance from husbands, from employers, and often from women themselves, Uncle Sam ultimately turned to the country's women for help. Recruiting women, many of whom had never worked before, to trade their familiar homesteads for aviation and munitions plants required outreach. And what better place to reach women than on the covers and pages of magazines? Beginning in 1942, the OWI's Magazine Bureau, headed by Dorothy Ducas, a journalist and friend of Eleanor Roosevelt's, distributed the *Magazine War Guide* to let editors and writers know the themes the government wanted stressed. The bureau provided information and suggested stories to editors at *Harper's Bazaar*, *Woman's Day*, *Cosmopolitan*, the *Saturday Evening Post*, and more. In September 1943, the *Magazine War Guide* even recommended that magazines take part in a "Women at Work Cover Promotion," depicting the array of work that women could do to support the war.

While previously, working women were depicted negatively in popular culture, in magazines and posters of the 1940s, they were glamorous, important, and—above all else—patriotic. One of the most enduring images of women's participation in the war effort is Rosie the Riveter. What many think of as the original image—featuring a woman in a red bandanna, sleeve rolled up, under the powerful slogan "We Can Do It!"—was actually created in

Don't Let That Shadow Touch Them *Buy* WAR BONDS

Mothers of Men— Build strong bodies

NUTRITION AND CANTEEN CLASSES

AMERICAN RED CROSS

OPPOSITE President Franklin Delano Roosevelt and his mother, Sara, at the Roosevelt estate in Hyde Park, New York, 1933. **ABOVE LEFT** A US war-bonds poster, featuring a Nazi swastika shadow superimposed on three children, 1942. **ABOVE RIGHT** A Red Cross poster appealing to "Mothers of Men," c. 1943.

FIND YOUR WAR JOB
In Industry – Agriculture – Business

"The more women at work,
the sooner we win."

—*World War II propaganda poster*

ABOVE LEFT Possibly the most well-known World War II–era poster today, "We Can Do It!" by J. Howard Miller was displayed for two weeks at Westinghouse's Midwest helmet-liner factories for morale. The poster was rediscovered in the 1980s and became a prominent symbol of the women's movement. ABOVE RIGHT A women's labor recruitment ad issued by the OWI, c.1944. OPPOSITE Eleanor Roosevelt and Dorothy Ducas in Hyde Park, New York, 1957.

1943 for the Westinghouse Electric Company by artist J. Howard Miller and not widely seen outside the companys's Midwest factories. Later, Norman Rockwell, possibly inspired by the 1942 song "Rosie the Riveter" by Redd Evans and John Jacob Loeb, created another image of Rosie for the May 29, 1943, cover of the *Saturday Evening Post*. In this now-famous image, "Rosie" is portrayed as a brawny, muscular woman in overalls, with a rivet machine on her lap, a ham sandwich in her hand, and her foot on a copy of *Mein Kampf*, as the American flag fills out the background. Rockwell's Rosie is a proud patriot, reminding America of women's contribution to the war effort.

Dorothy Ducas (1905–87)

When it came to the public's perception of what it meant to be a "working woman" during wartime, few people were as influential as Dorothy Ducas. A graduate of Columbia University, Mrs. Dorothy Ducas Herzog—who wrote under the name Dorothy Ducas—joined the *Saturday Evening Post* in 1927 and was later an editor for *McCall's* magazine. She was also the first woman to win a Pulitzer Traveling Scholarship.

During the war, she became chief of the Office of War Information's Magazine Bureau. Believing magazines to be of enormous influence with the reading public, especially women, she and her staff answered hundreds of letters from editors and writers a month requesting background information for stories, suggested articles to specific writers and editors, and appealed for "womanpower" to meet the needs of wartime production.

Like many working mothers of the time, she experienced the difficulties of balancing work and family. On December 8, 1943, Ducas left her position to spend more time with her family, stating, "I don't think I am irreplaceable in this work, but I am irreplaceable at home." She later served as public relations director for the March of Dimes and continued to write magazine articles and books. She died in 1987, leaving behind two sons and six grandchildren.

OPPOSITE A woman works on a B-25 bomber motor at a plant in Inglewood, California, 1942. ABOVE Women training at the Daytona Beach branch of the Volusia County, Florida, vocational school, 1942. TOP RIGHT Naval Air Station Corpus Christi, 1942. BOTTOM LEFT Two women in training for aircraft-engine installation at Douglas Aircraft Company, Long Beach, California, 1942. BOTTOM RIGHT A riveter at Lockheed Aircraft Corporation, Burbank, California, c. 1943

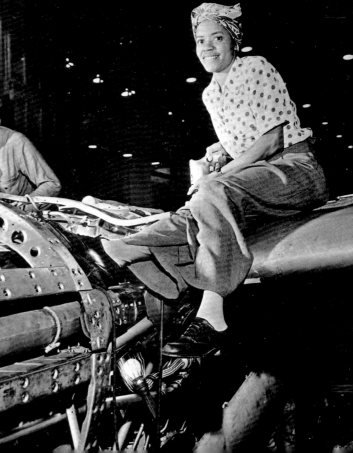

Advertising During Wartime

Advertising during World War II was not without challenges. Rubber and fuel were rationed, and with factories devoted to making the weapons of war, there just weren't as many consumer goods available. But that didn't stop the resourceful advertising industry, which appealed to mothers' patriotism to sell everything from soda to soup. One Campbell ad noted that their new and improved vegetable soup conformed with "the Government's wartime requirements calling for soups of higher food value and more nourishment"—encouraging moms to buy it "for vim and vigor and victory!" Other ads sought to quell women's qualms of conscience when it came to buying beauty products. An advertisement in the monthly publication *Click* insisted "War won't freeze American beauty" and reassured readers "if Uncle Sam needed your lipstick or shaving mug for bombs and bullets, he'd have gotten it first."

Other advertisers decided to look past the war, giving women a glimpse of the "kitchens of tomorrow" and preparing moms for post-war consumerism. As media news source *Ad Age*

summarizes, these ads "suggested all the stylish, modern, time-saving products that consumers would be able to buy once the conflict ended." Forward-thinking prototypes depicted in advertisements told housewives they would soon be able to "have it all," with modern technology that could accomplish everything from eliminating pots and pans to doing away with the need for women to stoop and squat in the kitchen. A famous "kitchen of

tomorrow" was developed in 1942–44 by industrial designer H. Creston Doner for the Libbey-Owens-Ford Glass Company. This inspirational kitchen appeared in magazines and newspapers, and full-scale models were displayed in department stores across the country. According to these campaigns, while moms toiled with the demands of running a household (and often working) during war, a life of convenience and luxury awaited after its conclusion.

When the war did end, wartime technologies led to new products advertisers could promote to mothers, including nylon, plastics, and Styrofoam®, synthetic detergents, and more. And, of course, as soldiers and working women returned home, a baby boom followed, leading to many new mothers in need of domestic goods for their families.

OPPOSITE This patriotic mother ad for Baby Ruth® appeared in the January 16, 1943, edition of the *Saturday Evening Post*. **ABOVE** The futuristic "kitchen of tomorrow" as seen in *Life* magazine, 1943.

"Never underestimate the power of a woman."
—Ladies' Home Journal *slogan, 1940s*

SEVEN

The Good Housewife

THE 1950s

"No one in the world can take the place of your mother.
Right or wrong, from her viewpoint you are always right."

—President Harry S. Truman

W ITH THEIR HUSBANDS returning from war, many women left the workforce and returned to their domestic spheres. Marriage rates were on the rise, and the nuclear family was depicted as an ideal contrast to communism—placing mothers and the American family on the front lines of the Cold War, the fraught relationship that developed between the United States and the USSR after World War II. As America experienced a new baby boom and a rising middle class, advertisers continued to reach out to moms—often using the new medium of television, which depicted mothers in contented, traditional roles on shows such as *Leave It to Beaver* and *Father Knows Best*. And yet, despite the image of the "happy homemaker"—an image of the '50s wife and mother that still prevails today—the reality was that many wives and mothers continued to pursue opportunities outside the home.

OPPOSITE The idealized "happy housewife" of the 1950s, as depicted in what was likely an ad in a women's magazine, c. 1955.

Now Buy This!

Between 1945 and 1964, America saw a dramatic baby boom, which resulted in a rise in homeownership with many families buying cars and settling in the suburbs. According to the US Census Bureau, homeownership rose from 55 percent in 1950 to 61.9 percent in 1960. The marriage rate in the '50s was at an all-time high, with couples marrying at young ages—the average age of marriage for women being twenty. These young women now had appliances to purchase, kitchens to stock, and babies to raise—and the money to do so. American advertisers didn't miss their chance to market their wares to the new, suburban, middle-class mom and housewife.

"God could not be everywhere, so he made mothers." —*Jewish proverb*

Advertisers promoted traditional family values, focusing on nuclear families enjoying consumer products and time together in their new homes and cars. Television was the hot new medium for advertisers, who initially produced TV programs to promote their brands. Print advertisements in newspapers and magazines were filled with images of the idealized American mom, who, despite having a plethora of time-saving appliances and products at her disposal, appeared to be busier than ever, sewing the latest fashions, searching for the tastiest and thriftiest meals, caring for her sick children, and baking the perfect delicacies—all before her husband returned home from his day at the office.

With large supermarket chains spreading into the suburbs, moms were inundated with food ads promising everything from scientifically balanced baking powder to delicious five-minute dinners—and the latest high-tech refrigerators in which to store them. Aspirin ads depicted mothers seeking out doctor-approved medicines to nurse their children back to health. Even beloved parents Ozzie and Harriet Nelson appeared in an ad for Tide® detergent. As the number of products on the shelves continued to grow, so did the advertising dollars—and they continued to be directed squarely at the American mom.

OPPOSITE After the war, television ownership skyrocketed in America, and many TV ads were geared toward the main shopper in the family—Mom. Here, a General Electric ad for their new Model 805, complete with cabinet. ABOVE American advertisers targeted the new, suburban, middle-class mom and housewife with images such as this one.

OVERLEAF Detail from a Frigidaire® ad from the June 19, 1951, issue of the *Saturday Evening Post*.

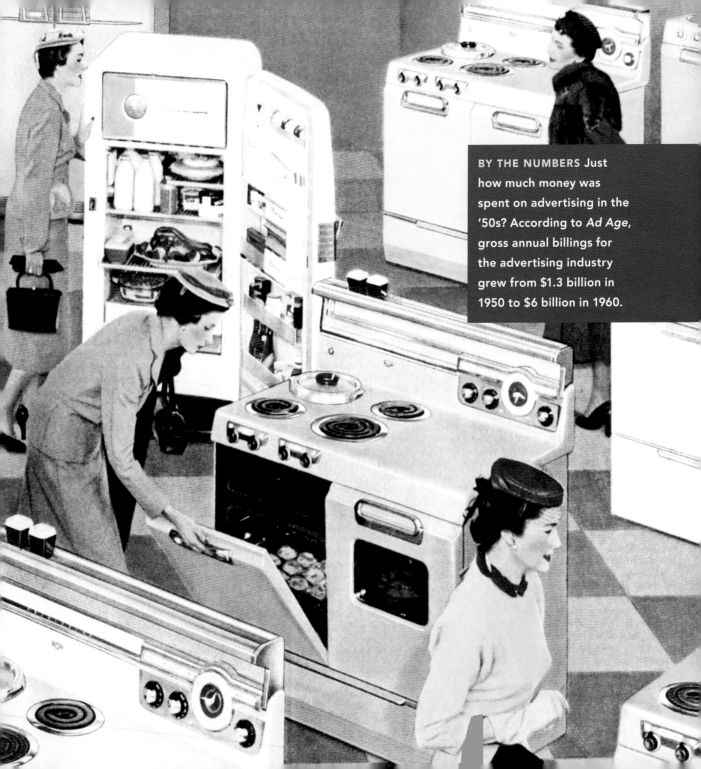

BY THE NUMBERS Just how much money was spent on advertising in the '50s? According to *Ad Age*, gross annual billings for the advertising industry grew from $1.3 billion in 1950 to $6 billion in 1960.

Working Moms and Desperate Housewives

As the '50s progressed, small changes began appearing on the covers and pages of magazines. While smiling, pearl-clad housewives dominated advertisements and the small screen, reality was often much different for American moms of the time. The Bureau of Labor Statistics reports that in 1950, 33.9 percent of women were in the labor force; by 1960, this participation had grown to 37.7 percent. According to *Time* magazine, a growing number of these women were mothers: In 1956, 16 percent of women with children under six worked outside the home. That same year, *Life* magazine published an issue dedicated to the American woman, with the cover featuring a working mother smiling lovingly at her child. The profiled working mom was portrayed as contributing extra money to the family and having a happy, fulfilling marriage.

For housewives, life at home wasn't always what it seemed. From behind newly purchased washing machines, dirty laundry began to surface, with couples' domestic problems airing in the *Ladies' Home Journal* column, "Can This Marriage Be Saved?" There were rumblings of a certain quiet malaise affecting the American housewife, emerging into the open in Betty Friedan's landmark 1960 *Good Housekeeping* article, "Women Are People, Too!" in which she described a "strange stirring" that eventually led to her groundbreaking 1963 book, *The Feminine Mystique*.

Sign of the Times

In the 1950s, moms on television and in magazines were fairly homogenous. But times were changing, and with the launch of magazines such as *Ebony* and *Jet*, aimed at African American readers, brands began to seek out wider markets. In 1955, Coca-Cola® featured its first female African American model, Mary Alexander. With ads portraying Alexander posed happily with a husband and son, suddenly family refreshment had a refreshingly new face.

Mary Alexander grew up on a farm in Alabama. While at Clark College in Atlanta, she auditioned to model for Coca-Cola, which was looking to recruit African Americans for a new campaign. She earned $600 for about fifteen ads, which was enough to pay for a year of college tuition. While she didn't continue her modeling career, she went on to earn a master's degree in education and became a teacher and a high school principal. Continuing to break new ground, Alexander was later named the first female African American director of vocational education for the state of Michigan.

The Perfect Moms of Television

The characters and storylines may have differed, but when it came to '50s family television, you could count on some things remaining the same: a gentle, nurturing mother

OPPOSITE Portrait of writer and feminist Betty Friedan, c. 1964.
ABOVE Before the Kardashians, there were the Nelsons—Rick, Dave, Harriet, and Ozzie—here, getting ready to watch their own show at home, c. 1960s.

smiling up from her strand of pearls, cooking for her family (in heels!), and gracefully guiding her children through whatever comedic teachable moments they encountered that week. While modern mothers may not resemble their '50s sitcom counterparts, those early TV moms still hold a special place in our hearts. In 2008 and 2013, the Harris Poll surveyed approximately 2,500 American adults on which TV moms they would most like to have had as their own when growing up, and the same winner emerged both times—June Cleaver, the beloved mom from *Leave It to Beaver*, followed by *The Cosby Show*'s Clair Huxtable and *The Brady Bunch*'s Carol Brady. Here are a few of the most popular sitcom moms of the '50s:

HARRIET NELSON, *The Adventures of Ozzie and Harriet* This drama based on a real-life family began on the radio in 1944, before moving to television in 1952 and running for an astounding fourteen seasons. Blending TV and reality, the show followed Harriet and Ozzie Nelson and their sons David and Ricky, basing many of the episodes on the family's everyday problems. Their fictional home was even modeled to look like their actual family home in southern California (see page 87). Despite this unusual approach, the Nelson family was rather traditional. Harriet Nelson had given up a rather colorful career as a nightclub and radio singer to star as a housewife—a transition familiar to many women of the '50s who left their (albeit less glamorous) jobs to take on the new roles of wife and mother.

MARGARET ANDERSON (JANE WYATT), *Father Knows Best* This popular sitcom also began on the radio in 1949 before it made the switch to television in 1954. The show follows Jim Anderson (Robert Young) and his wife, Margaret, loving parents raising three children in a midwestern town: Betty (Elinor Donahue), Bud (Billy Gray), and Kathy (Lauren Chapin). Jim works in insurance while Margaret is a housewife, portrayed as calm and patient, serving as a voice of reason in any family crisis. Whether she is cooking with her daughters, volunteering as a chaperone at the school dance, or speaking at PTA functions, Margaret Anderson is a consummate '50s wife and mother.

JUNE CLEAVER (BARBARA BILLINGSLEY), *Leave It to Beaver* Released in 1957, *Leave It to Beaver* followed the boyhood adventures and mishaps of Theodore "The Beaver" Cleaver (Jerry Mathers) and his big brother, Wally (Tony Dow), who live in a nice suburban house with their happily married parents, June and Ward Cleaver (Hugh Beaumont). In this idyllic picture of '50s life, Ward works at an office, while June stays home with the boys, enjoying needlepoint and reading magazines in her spare time. She cooks and bakes for her family, has endless patience with her often messy and mischievous son Beaver, and is perpetually well-dressed and composed. Who wouldn't want June Cleaver as their mother?

LUCY RICARDO (LUCILLE BALL), *I Love Lucy*
Voted the "Best TV Show of All Time" in a 2012 survey conducted by ABC News and *People* magazine, *I Love Lucy* starred the dynamic and beloved Lucille Ball as Lucy Ricardo, the wife of a Cuban American musician, Ricky Ricardo, played by Desi Arnaz—Ball's husband in real life. The show debuted in 1951 and depicted the first interracial marriage on an American TV show. Unlike many of the other TV wives, Lucy was a distinctly comedic character—a feisty troublemaker, a homemaker with aspirations to be a performer, and, after the second season, a new mother, stunning America when it was revealed both the character and the actress were expecting.

DONNA STONE (DONNA REED), *The Donna Reed Show* *The Donna Reed Show* is a classic of the mid-twentieth century, centering around Donna Stone, the attractive and wise wife of pediatrician Alex Stone (Carl

Betz) and mother of two teenagers, Jeff (Paul Petersen) and Mary (Shelley Fabares). The show ran from 1958 to 1966, and was coproduced by Donna Reed's then-husband, Tony Owen. Donna Reed's character kept a pristine house, was happily married and involved in the community, and managed her family with a humor and grace that appealed to '50s housewives—and still makes modern viewers nostalgic for a "simpler" time.

OPPOSITE Jerry Mathers and Barbara Billingsley as Beaver and June Cleaver in a still from *Leave It to Beaver*, c. 1958. ABOVE Paul Petersen, Carl Betz, and Donna Reed, in a c. 1959 scene from *The Donna Reed Show*.

> "We really don't care what it is, but as long as we already have a girl it would be nice to have a boy. I'll have one on television anyway."
>
> —*Lucille Ball*

RIGHT Lucy tries swaddling a baby doll in the December 15, 1952, episode of *I Love Lucy*; the episode aired a week after "Lucy Is Enceinte" and was surprisingly titled "Pregnant Women Are Unpredictable," possibly because episode titles were not shown onscreen. OPPOSITE The Ball-Arnaz family on the cover of *Look* magazine, December 28, 1954.

"Lucy Is Enceinte"! Pregnancy and Pop Culture

It was 1952, and the star of America's most beloved sitcom was . . . expecting. CBS executives, having decided to work Lucille Ball's second pregnancy into the season, were still queasy about certain aspects of her on-screen pregnancy—specifically, about the use of the word *pregnant*, which no one was allowed to say on the show. (Hence the use of the French word *enceinte* in the title of the episode, which aired on December 8, 1952.) When it came to relations between

"It's a boy. . . . Now we have everything."

—Desi Arnaz

husbands and wives, '50s television was still rather conservative. While Lucy wasn't the first pregnant character on TV, featuring a story arc of a real-time pregnancy was a groundbreaking move for the popular program—with some reports that a priest, a minister, and a rabbi were called upon to approve the "Lucy Is Enceinte" script before the network would proceed. Lucille Ball's—and Lucy Ricardo's—condition was still rather delicate for TV.

Lucy fans, however, didn't seem to mind. When the episode "Lucy Goes to the Hospital" aired on January 19, 1953, more than 71 percent of American television sets were tuned in to see the birth of Little Ricky—timed to coincide with the birth of Lucille Ball and husband Desi Arnaz's own baby, Desi Jr. In fact, more people watched the birth of Little Ricky on television than the inauguration of Dwight Eisenhower as president of the United States the next day! The publicity-savvy stars of *I Love Lucy* scheduled the cesarean birth of their son to coincide with the birth of Little Ricky on TV.

Lucy may have received all the publicity, but she wasn't the first sitcom mom to be pregnant on TV. Television's first situation comedy, *Mary Kay and Johnny,* premiered on November 18, 1947, on the DuMont Network. The show, which was broadcast live and aired in fifteen-minute episodes, was written and based on quirky real-life New York City newlyweds Mary Kay and Johnny Stearns. The show wasn't afraid to push boundaries, and was the first of its kind to show a married couple sharing a bed. When Mary Kay became pregnant in real life, the producers first tried to hide it; when that no longer worked, they incorporated the pregnancy into the show. On December 19, 1948, Mary Kay gave birth to baby Christopher, who weeks later joined the cast.

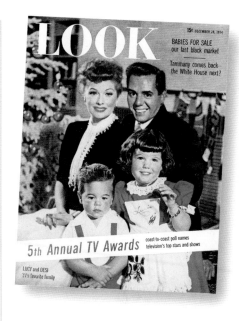

BY THE NUMBERS
When "Lucy Goes to the "Hospital" aired, 44 million viewers watched the episode. A "mere" 29 million viewers watched President Eisenhower's inauguration the following day.

SHOWERED WITH LOVE

While today baby showers are common affairs, rituals surrounding birth go back thousands of years. In ancient Egypt and Greece, mothers and newborns were briefly secluded away from the rest of the community, due to concerns about "impurities" surrounding the birth process. In the Victorian era, while women were encouraged to conceal their "delicate condition" and avoid taboo words like *pregnancy*, they were treated to a tea party after the baby's birth. Today, this party has transformed into a joyous social rite—the baby shower—with elaborate registries and even the occasional corporate sponsorship.

With showers such a popular part of American culture, it's no wonder they've become a mainstay on American TV. Who can forget the baby shower for '90s mother-to-be Murphy Brown (Candice Bergen), whose sitcom shower was attended by real-life journalists Katie Couric, Mary Alice Williams, Paula Zahn, Faith Daniels, and Joan Lunden? A decade later, millions watched the shower for *Friends'* Rachel Green (Jennifer Aniston), where she panicked about not being prepared for motherhood. Over the years, sitcom showers have created opportunities for unexpected cameos, humorous plot twists, and confessions about expectant mothers'

ABOVE A cast photo from the star-studded baby shower episode of *Murphy Brown*, which aired May 11, 1992. From left to right—standing, back row: Faith Ford, Faith Daniels, Joan Lunden, Katie Couric; seated, front: Mary Alice Williams, Candice Bergen, Paula Zahn. **OPPOSITE** Host Heidi Klum at *Operation Shower*, sponsored by Babies"R"Us, held in the Globe Theatre at Universal Studios, March 4, 2014, in Universal City, California.

deepest anxieties surrounding motherhood—themes that resonate with their expecting viewers.

And then, of course, there's the celebrity shower. Today's tabloids are filled with photos of upscale baby showers featuring familiar faces—and some equally familiar brands. For example, in 2016, reality stars Catherine and Sean Lowe, of ABC's *The Bachelor*, were thrown a "Loads of Love" baby shower in New York City by baby detergent brand Dreft®. In 2014, *Operation Shower*, which hosts showers for expecting military moms, was joined by supermodel fashion designer Heidi Klum and Babies"R"Us® to throw a shower for 125 moms-to-be. Talk about a big registry!

"We never know the love of a parent
until we become parents ourselves."

—Henry Ward Beecher

EIGHT

Winds of Change

THE 1960s

*"If you bungle raising your children,
I don't think whatever else you do matters very much."*

—Jacqueline Kennedy Onassis

THE 1960s WERE a time of dynamic change in America. Against the backdrop of the civil rights movement, the Vietnam War, and a rising counterculture, the roots of modern-day feminism began to emerge. In her landmark 1963 book *The Feminine Mystique*, Betty Friedan wrote, "the problem that has no name burst like a boil through the image of the happy American housewife." Indeed, more women than ever before were venturing outside the home into the workforce—by the end of the '60s, women made up around 37 percent of the US labor force. Things were changing inside the bedroom as well; with the rising popularity of the Pill, by the decade's end, more than 80 percent of wives were using contraception. Mothers were experiencing newfound freedoms—planning families, pursuing careers, and, in a decade of often-turbulent transformation, seeking to make the world a better place for their children.

OPPOSITE A baby sleeps peacefully while her mother marches in a ban-the-bomb protest outside the United Nations in New York, 1962.

Changing Channels

The '60s saw a new generation of TV moms enter America's living rooms. While these mothers continued to care for their families as stay-at-home moms, a few changes were noticeable. For one thing, the traditional uniform of pearls, heels, and dressy skirts was replaced by—somewhat shockingly—pants. On *The Dick Van Dyke Show* (1961–66), Laura Petrie, played by Mary Tyler Moore, was one of the first TV moms to go about her day's activities in pants. When the show's young, attractive mother sported a pair of capri pants, it initially sparked concern with the show's sponsors. At first, Moore was limited to wearing pants in one scene per episode, a restriction that was quickly relaxed as viewing audiences seemed to accept the wardrobe choice—a realistic representation that mimicked how moms actually dressed inside their homes.

The Brady Bunch first aired in 1969 and hinted at a changing time. Carol Brady, played by Florence Henderson, was a stay-at-home mother, but she was undeniably more modern than many of her TV predecessors. She dressed in the latest "groovy" fashions, including pants. She was also part of a blended family, remarrying and building a new family with her new husband, Mike (played by Robert Reed), his three sons, and her three daughters. While Mike was a widower, it was left ambiguous whether Carol was a widow or a divorcée— supposedly because the network wasn't comfortable depicting her as the latter. And unlike earlier TV housewives, Carol Brady wasn't burdened with the tedium of cooking and laundry—she had Alice, the housekeeper, to do those tasks, freeing her up to pursue her own interests, such as going out with her husband and solving the problems of six children in thirty minutes.

FUN FACT While Mary Tyler Moore's capri pants caused some controversy at the time, Laura Petrie was not the only—or even the most famous—sitcom housewife to don pants on TV. Lucy Ricardo, played by Lucille Ball, frequently wore pants on *I Love Lucy.*

LEFT A colorized still of Mary Tyler Moore in capri pants as Laura Petrie, showing off her dance moves in an episode of *The Dick Van Dyke Show* that aired December 26, 1962. **OPPOSITE** The Brady clan poses on the staircase of their house on set; Florence Henderson as the groovy mom Carol Brady is second from right.

Morticia Addams

While June Cleaver and Carol Brady may come to mind as the typical classic TV moms, fans of the cult classic *The Addams Family* (1964–66) hold a special place in their heart for the show's matriarch, Morticia Addams. Played by Carolyn Jones, Morticia was, in many ways, a far cry from the usual '50s or '60s housewife. With her gothic appearance and love of the macabre, she followed her own rules and had no regard for what others thought of her or her family. She voiced her opinions, was direct with her children, and pursued her own interests, from creating potions to cutting the blooms off roses to arrange the stems as decorations. And yet, in other ways, she was a traditional TV mother: She cared deeply for her children, was fiercely protective of her family, and was passionately in love with her husband. *The Addams Family*, created by cartoonist Charles Addams and originally published in the *New Yorker*, proves that a mother's love doesn't change—whether that mother is clad in pearls and pushing a vacuum cleaner or attired in black and talking to a disembodied hand.

"Families are like fudge . . . mostly sweet with a few nuts."

—*Unknown*

Revisiting the '60s Mom

The '60s may have been a tumultuous time for those who lived through it, between the draft and the Vietnam War, the counterculture movement, and the fight for civil rights, but the decade continues to capture the imaginations of film and television producers to this day. Shows and movies continue to flash back to when flowers were groovy and bellbottoms were couture, and the '60s American mom continues to rise from the past in her full glory—for viewers to love, criticize, and wonder, "Is she really smoking cigarettes in front of the kids?"

One of the most popular recent representations of a '60s mom is Betty Draper (played by January Jones) from AMC's drama *Mad Men*, which aired on AMC from 2007 to 2015. Betty is the housewife who on the surface has it all—a handsome, successful husband; beautiful children; a big house in the suburbs—but is dissatisfied and searching for a fulfillment that neither she nor her therapist can name. Admittedly, she's

OPPOSITE Carolyn Jones, center, played the elegantly goth mom Morticia Addams in *The Addams Family*; the show only ran from 1964 to 1966, but it became a cult classic that spawned several reboots and feature films. **LEFT** January Jones was riveting as the conflicted housewife Betty Draper on *Mad Men*. She is shown here in a 2008 episode with her TV children, Bobby (Aaron Hart) and Sally (Kiernan Shipka).

not mother of the year, but with her societal limitations and pre–*Feminine Mystique* sensibilities, she's very much a product of her time.

The Wonder Years, on ABC from 1988 to 1993, was a late '60s-era coming-of-age series featuring a less controversial mom, Norma Arnold. While Norma (played by Alley Mills) deferred to her husband on most things, she sought to understand her flower-child daughter and, with her caring and patience, was at the heart of the Arnold clan. And after her husband's death, she became a businesswoman and board chairman, achieving her own career ambitions in a more open-minded time.

Yet perhaps no '60s family inspires more Hollywood and small-screen remakes than the Kennedys. Jackie Kennedy and her iconic fashions have been portrayed by actresses from Gilda Radner on *Saturday Night Live* in 1977, to Natalie Portman in the 2016 biopic film *Jackie*. The famous First Lady and devoted mother has not only been reinvented comedically and seriously, but also rather unexpectedly, in sci-fi series such as *Dark Skies* and *Timequest*. While she was First Lady for only a short time, decades later there is no shortage of award-winning actresses clamoring to play the elegant and legendary widow of President John F. Kennedy.

ABOVE LEFT Actress Alley Mills (second from left) as the lovable mom in *The Wonder Years*, along with her cast family Jason Hervey, Olivia d'Abo, Fred Savage, and Dan Lauria.   **ABOVE RIGHT** Natalie Portman, as First Lady Jacqueline Kennedy, dances with Caspar Phillipson, as President John F. Kennedy, in the 2016 film *Jackie*.   **OPPOSITE** President John F. Kennedy applauds his mother, Rose Kennedy, at a Kennedy foundation banquet, June 12, 1962.

Rose Kennedy

Mother of John F. Kennedy

Rose Elizabeth Fitzgerald Kennedy (1890–1995) was the mother of several of America's most famous politicians. The oldest of six children, she was born into a political Massachusetts family, as her father, John F. Fitzgerald, was a congressman and mayor of Boston. In 1914, she married Joseph Patrick Kennedy—later a US ambassador to Britain—and shortly after the marriage she gave birth to the couple's first child, Joseph Jr. Eight more children followed: John, Rosemary, Kathleen, Eunice, Patricia, Robert, Jean, and Ted. A strict Catholic, she was actively involved in charities and women's groups. In 1951, the Vatican bestowed on her the title of papal countess for her "exemplary motherhood and many charitable works." She died at the age of 104 at the family compound at Hyannis Port, Massachusetts.

> "I looked at child rearing not only as a work of love and duty, but as a profession that was as fully interesting and challenging as any honorable profession in the world."
>
> —*Rose Kennedy*

> ## "I'll be a wife and mother first, then First Lady."
> —*Jacqueline Kennedy*

JACQUELINE KENNEDY ONASSIS
(First Lady 1961–63)

Born in Southampton, New York, in 1929, Jackie Kennedy graduated from George Washington University with a degree in French literature, after which she briefly worked as a photographer for the *Washington Times-Herald*. In 1952, she met Massachusetts congressman John F. Kennedy, whom she married a year later. The couple's first child, Caroline, was born in 1957; Jackie gave birth to John F. Kennedy Jr. shortly after her husband's presidential election in 1960. Photos at the time captured joyful moments between the First Lady and her young children, reading to them or horseback riding.

As First Lady, she traveled often and restored the historical character of the White House. In early 1963, she gave birth to a third child, Patrick, who died two days later; in November of that same year, her husband was assassinated. She later married Aristotle Onassis and worked in book publishing after his death. She died in 1994, at age sixty-four.

Moms in the White House

While the White House has been home to America's most famous leaders, it's also housed a considerable number of mothers who've raised their children in some pretty unusual circumstances. Here's a look at just a few of the famous mothers who resided at 1600 Pennsylvania Avenue since the 1960s.

ABOVE The Kennedy family relaxes in Hyannisport, Massachusetts, August 14, 1963. John F. Kennedy Jr. and his sister Caroline play with the family dogs. OPPOSITE First Lady Betty Ford and her daughter, Susan, make Christmas ornaments in the White House Solarium, November 10, 1975.

Betty Ford *(First Lady 1974–77)*

Born in Chicago in 1918, Betty Ford grew up in Grand Rapids, Michigan. After high school she studied dance with famed choreographer Martha Graham, supporting herself by modeling. She joined Graham's auxiliary dance company, with whom she performed at Carnegie Hall. In 1948, she married lawyer and World War II veteran Gerald Ford, her second marriage after a previous divorce. The couple went on to have four children: Michael, John, Steven, and Susan.

Betty Ford was a Cub Scout den mother and Sunday school teacher and made it a point not to spank or hit her children. She was also known for her candor. Appearing in 1975 on *60 Minutes*, she discussed how she would respond if her daughter told her she were having an affair and mused that her children may have experimented with marijuana. She is perhaps best known for founding the Betty Ford Center in California, a treatment center for drug and alcohol addiction, after bravely overcoming her own battles with addiction. She died in 2011 at age ninety-three.

"It's always been my feeling that God lends you your children until they're about eighteen years old. If you haven't made your points with them by then, it's too late." —*Betty Ford*

> "We have learned that to raise a happy, healthy, and hopeful child . . . takes all of us. Yes, it takes a village."
>
> —*Hillary Rodham Clinton,*
> *Democratic National Convention, 1996*

HILLARY RODHAM CLINTON *(First Lady 1993–2001)* Hillary Rodham Clinton was born in 1947 in Chicago. She graduated from Wellesley College and Yale Law School, where she caught the eye of fellow student William Jefferson Clinton. In 1975, Hillary and Bill Clinton married and settled in Arkansas. Five years later, Hillary Clinton gave birth to their only child, Chelsea.

A partner at an Arkansas law firm, Hillary became the state's First Lady when her husband was elected governor and then First Lady of the United States in 1993. Known for being an especially involved First Lady, in 2000 she became the first female US senator of New York. After campaigning unsuccessfully for president against Barack Obama in 2008, she went on to become his secretary of state. Hillary made another unsuccessful bid for president as the 2016 Democratic Party nominee, the first woman ever to be nominated by a major party. Chelsea Clinton, herself a married mother at the time, helped her mother campaign for president during both runs and even introduced her at both the 2008 Democratic National Convention in Denver and the 2016 convention in Philadelphia.

BELOW President Bill Clinton and Chelsea Clinton celebrate in New York City with First Lady Hillary Rodham Clinton after her win for New York State Senate, November 7, 2000. **OPPOSITE** President George W. Bush and Mrs. Laura Bush pose with daughters Jenna and Barbara at Prairie Chapel Ranch in Crawford, Texas, prior to the wedding of Jenna and Henry Hager, May 10, 2008.

LAURA BUSH *(First Lady 2001–9)*

Born in 1946 in Midland, Texas, Laura Bush earned a bachelor's degree in early education from Southern Methodist University. She taught second grade before receiving her master's in library science and becoming a public school librarian. In July 1977, she met George W. Bush, son of forty-first president George H. W. Bush, and the two were married four months later. Laura Bush gave birth to twins Jenna and Barbara in 1981.

Laura Bush became the First Lady of Texas in 1995 after her husband successfully ran for governor, and then First Lady of the United States in 2001. After the events of September 11 that year, Laura Bush found herself having to comfort a nation, addressing anxious parents and families trying to make sense of the tragedy. Passionate about educational issues, in 2002 she testified on Capitol Hill on the importance of early childhood education. She supported many women's health and wellness initiatives, traveling the country to raise women's awareness of heart disease, promoting breast-cancer screening and research, and encouraging HIV testing. In 2007, the Laura W. Bush Institute for Women's Health was established at Texas Tech University, with the goal of promoting research and encouraging community programs and health screenings. As First Lady, she also traveled to Afghanistan and championed the rights of women in that country through the US-Afghan Women's Council. In 2008, she and her daughter Jenna Bush cowrote a children's book, *Read All About It!*

"As parents, the most important thing we can do is read to our children early and often."

—*Laura Bush*

Determined to put her daughters first, during her husband's presidential run she limited her time away campaigning to one overnight trip per week. She still, however, had an enormous influence on his campaign, delivering a powerful speech at the 2008 Democratic National Convention in Denver, Colorado. As First Lady, she focused on families and children, with her initiatives including advocating on behalf of military families, helping working women to balance career and family, and promoting arts education. Concerned about child obesity, she launched the "Let's Move!" initiative, urging kids to be more physically active, and planted an organic vegetable garden at the White House. In 2016, she delivered a groundbreaking speech in support of presidential candidate Hillary Clinton at the Democratic National Convention in Philadelphia.

"For me, being Mom-in-Chief is, and always will be, job number one."

—*Michelle Obama*

MICHELLE OBAMA *(First Lady 2009–17)*

Michelle Obama was born in Chicago in 1964. She earned her bachelor's degree in sociology from Princeton University, going on to receive a law degree from Harvard. While working at a Chicago law firm, she was asked to mentor a summer associate named Barack Obama. The two married in 1992, and Michelle Obama later gave birth to two daughters, Malia and Natasha (known as "Sasha").

ABOVE First Lady Michelle Obama, President Barack Obama, and their daughters, Malia, left, and Sasha, right, sit for a family portrait by Pete Souza in the Oval Office, December 11, 2011. **OPPOSITE** Tireless fighter for workers' rights and child labor laws Mary Harris "Mother" Jones, c. 1912.

MUCKRAKING MOMS

The '60s saw the rise of some of America's most famous political activists. But some American moms were agitating for change decades before organized protests hit the evening TV news. From union organizers to champions of clean water, here are just a few moms-turned-muckrakers throughout American history.

MARY HARRIS JONES (1837–1930), more popularly known as "Mother Jones," was born in County Cork, Ireland, and immigrated to Canada and eventually the United States. In 1867, the schoolteacher and dressmaker lost her husband and four young children to yellow fever. In an attempt to rebuild her life, she moved to Chicago and opened a dress shop—which burned to the ground in the Great Chicago Fire of 1871. After this loss, she organized strikes for the Knights of Labor and the United Mine Workers. She fought against child labor and for men to make a decent wage, so mothers could stay home and raise their children. In 1903, she organized a march of children working in Pennsylvania's silk mills. Jones was sentenced to prison several times, and denounced on the floor of the US Senate as the "grandmother of all agitators." She died in 1930 and is buried in the Union Miners Cemetery in Mount Olive, Illinois. The progressive magazine *Mother Jones*, founded in 1976, is named after her.

> "I hope to live long enough to be the great-grandmother of all agitators."
>
> —*Mother Jones*

MARY CHURCH TERRELL (1863–1954), born in Memphis, Tennessee, to former slaves, was a founding member of the National Association for the Advancement of Colored People and one of the first African American women to earn a college degree. She married lawyer Robert Heberton Terrell in 1891, and the couple had three children who died in infancy, a surviving daughter, Phyllis, and an adopted daughter, Mary. She met Frederick Douglass and Booker T. Washington, and worked with Douglass on various civil rights campaigns. Terrell also served as president of the National Association of Colored Women, founded the National Association of College Women, was active in the women's suffrage movement, and was the first black woman appointed to the District of Columbia Board of Education.

CORETTA SCOTT KING (1927–2006), the wife of Martin Luther King Jr. and mother of four, was a human rights activist and leader of the civil rights movement. Born in Marion, Alabama, she studied at Antioch College in Ohio and the New England Conservatory of Music in Boston, where she met Martin Luther King Jr. The couple married in 1953 and moved to Montgomery, Alabama, where he became pastor of the Dexter Avenue Baptist Church. Together with her husband, she took part

in the Montgomery Bus Boycott, worked for the passage of the Civil Rights Act, and traveled the world advocating for racial and economic justice. A trained musician, she performed Freedom Concerts as fundraisers for the Southern Christian Leadership Conference. After her husband's assassination, Coretta Scott King founded the Martin Luther King Jr. Center for Nonviolent Social Change in Atlanta.

ERIN BROCKOVICH's story was brought to life in an award-winning performance by Julia Roberts. Born in 1960 in Lawrence, Kansas, Brockovich briefly worked as a management trainee before entering and winning the Miss Pacific Coast beauty pageant in 1981. After that she moved to Reno, Nevada, where the twice-divorced mother of three was injured in a traffic accident that changed the course of her life. She began working as a file clerk at the law firm of her attorney, Ed Masry, leading to her investigation of a California utility company. Brockovich and Masry spearheaded a lawsuit alleging that the company had polluted the groundwater of a small town in southern California. In one of the largest direct-action lawsuit settlements in US history, the company paid out a $333 million settlement. She has since

been involved in other antipollution lawsuits, hosted TV series, and written a book, *Take It from Me: Life's a Struggle But You Can Win.*

Julia Roberts won an Oscar for Best Actress in a Leading Role portraying the activist in the 2000 movie *Erin Brockovich.* The film was also nominated for Best Picture, Best Actor in a Supporting Role, Best Director, and Best Writing, Screenplay Written Directly for the Screen.

OPPOSITE, LEFT Portrait of Mary Church Terrell, founding member of the NAACP and civil rights advocate, c. 1900.
OPPOSITE, RIGHT Coretta Scott King at the Democratic National Convention in New York, July 13, 1976.
ABOVE Antipollution crusader Erin Brockovich at a press conference in Florida, October 8, 2009.

NINE

Taking Care of Business

THE 1970s

"There is no undertaking more challenging, no responsibility
more awesome, than that of being a mother."

—PRESIDENT GERALD FORD

THE ROOTS OF FEMINISM that had been planted in the 1960s blossomed in the 1970s. Women were beginning to work outside the home in much larger numbers, including many married women and mothers. Women applied for jobs traditionally held by men, attended professional schools, and worked while pregnant. Laws gradually changed, allowing no-fault divorce and prohibiting sex-segregated job advertisements. Television and movies began to portray working and single moms, as well as African American mothers. Advertisers, while still appealing to housewives, began to reach out to working mothers as well. With more opportunities open to women—and greater social acceptance of these new roles—working moms faced a struggle to balance career and family that continues to the present day.

OPPOSITE In *One Day at a Time,* Bonnie Franklin (shown here with TV daughters Mackenzie Phillips and Valerie Bertinelli) as Ann Romano was one of the first portrayals of a single mom on the small screen,

ABOVE Bea Arthur (as Maude Findlay) and Esther Rolle (as Florida Evans) in *Maude*; Esther Rolle went on to star in her own series, *Good Times*, based on the same character. **OPPOSITE** Meryl Streep and Justin Henry as mother and son in *Kramer vs. Kramer*, 1979.

The New Faces of Motherhood

Americans turning on the television or watching movies during the '70s noticed something different about Mom. Yes, housewives still abounded, but a new type of mom was emerging as well. This mom worked outside the home and was sometimes even single, raising her children on her own as a divorcée or widow. African American mothers appeared as centers of family life, such as Florida Evans (played by Esther Rolle), the Chicago mother of three on *Good Times* (1974–79). Florida, who started out as a housekeeper on the sitcom *Maude* (1972–78), was a stay-at-home mom who eventually had to support her family after the death of her first husband. On *Maude*, the title character, played by Bea Arthur, was herself an unusual character—an outspoken grandmother married to her fourth husband, whose daughter, Carol (played by Adrienne Barbeau), was herself a divorced single mother. On *One Day at a Time* (1975–84), Bonnie Franklin played divorced mother Ann Romano, who was raising two teenage daughters, Barbara (Valerie Bertinelli) and Julie (Mackenzie Phillips) (see page 110).

On the big screen, Martin Scorsese's 1974 film *Alice Doesn't Live Here Anymore* followed Ellen Burstyn as a widow who travels across the country with her son to pursue a singing career, eventually working as a waitress to support him. And the heart-wrenching 1979 *Kramer vs. Kramer* centered around a divorce and bitter custody battle between Dustin Hoffman and Meryl Streep, earning Academy Awards for the film, its actors, and its director, Stanley R. Jaffe.

These representations mirrored trends in the off-screen roles of mothers. The number of women working outside the home skyrocketed during the '70s. In 1975, the labor participation rate for mothers with children under eighteen years of age was 47.4 percent; by 1980, it surpassed 56 percent. Single motherhood was also on the rise in the '70s and '80s. According to the Pew Research Center, in 1970, 11 percent of births were to unmarried mothers; by 1990, that number had risen to 28 percent. By 2014, that rate had risen to 41 percent. While TV and movies still often depicted mothers in traditional roles, they couldn't ignore the changing faces of modern motherhood—creating beloved, realistic characters who resonated with all mothers, no matter their home life or occupation.

BY THE NUMBERS
According to the US Department of Labor, in 2013, almost 70 percent of mothers with children ages eighteen and younger participated in the labor force.

Enjoli - the new 8 hour perfume for the 24 hour woman. You can feed the kids and the gerbils. Pass out the kisses. And get to work by 5 of 9! You can work all day in the old rat race. Even put a smile on sourpuss' face! You can bring home the bacon. Fry it up in a pan. And never let him forget he's a man! Because you're a woman!

ENJOLI

Compliments of Charles of the Ritz

> "We must reject not only the stereotypes that others hold of us, but also the stereotypes that we hold of ourselves." —*Shirley Chisholm, 1970*

OPPOSITE One of the most iconic ads of the 1970s, for Enjoli, the "new 8 hour perfume for the 24 hour woman."

Selling to the Working Mom

While many advertisements in the '70s still targeted the traditional home-maker and mother, the advertising industry was slowly awakening to the possibility of selling products to working moms. Some ads touted the benefits of quick, convenient meals for working moms with little time to cook. Other ads even portrayed husbands taking care of children or cooking dinner. In addition, more women began to enter the advertising industry, bringing a broader view of women and motherhood to the creative process.

As women entered jobs previously held only by men, some companies sought to encourage public trust in their new workforce. One insurance ad asked, "Ever buy life insurance from a woman? Some of the best in the business represent New York Life." Similarly, in the early '70s, AT&T ran an ad depicting one of its first female phone installers.

Perhaps one of the most famous ads of the time was for the perfume Enjoli® by Charles of the Ritz®. This 1978 campaign presented the "superwoman" who could easily handle a career, care for her kids, and make her husband feel like a man. Based on the melody from the Jerry Leiber and Mike Stoller song "I'm a Woman"—which Peggy Lee made a hit in 1962—the confident star of the commercial sings, "I can bring home the bacon and fry it up in a pan." A new woman was emerging as the '80s approached, and she was a far cry from the dutiful '50s housewife. As the Virginia Slims® cigarette ad proclaimed to women consumers, "You've come a long way, baby!"

BY THE NUMBERS
Between 1973 and 1986, the number of women working in the advertising industry nearly tripled, according to *Ad Age*.

Lillian Carter

Mother of Jimmy Carter

Born in Georgia in 1898, Bessie Lillian Gordy was the fourth of nine children. She trained to be a nurse and in 1923 married James Earl Carter, who managed a farm supply store. The couple went on to have four children: Jimmy, Gloria, Ruth, and Billy. Lillian Carter worked as a nurse and often cared for black patients, inviting them to enter through the front door and visit in her parlor—all unconventional acts for a white woman at that time in the South.

When her husband died in 1953, Carter looked to involve herself in something new, and served as housemother at a fraternity at Auburn University in Alabama. In 1966, she volunteered, in her sixties, to go to India with the Peace Corps, where she assisted at a clinic outside of Bombay. When Jimmy Carter ran for president in 1976, she helped him with his campaign, making speeches and watching his daughter, Amy. During her son's presidency, she cowrote two books, *Miss Lillian and Friends* and *Away from Home: Letters to My Family*. Lillian Carter died in 1983 at the age of eighty-five.

> "If I had one wish for my children, it would be that each of you would dare to do the things and reach for goals in your own lives that have meaning for you as individuals."
>
> —*Lillian Carter, in a letter to her family while in India*

Magazines for a New Generation of Moms

With the momentum of the '70s feminist movement, it was only fitting that there was a woman-run magazine where women could express and explore issues that mattered to them. Feminists Gloria Steinem and Dorothy Pitman Hughes cofounded *Ms.* magazine as a magazine for women by women. It was first published as an insert in *New York Magazine* in 1971, and then as its own standalone issue in 1972. With articles ranging from domestic violence to raising kids without sex roles, *Ms.* covered controversial topics not typically represented in other publications. The magazine is still in print today, priding itself on giving expression to feminist journalism and voices.

In 1979, a new magazine entered the scene: *Working Mother*, a national magazine for moms balancing career and family. Early issues included headlines such as "How can you leave that baby?" and "My husband thinks much more of me now," and targeted mothers working for extra household money or returning to work. The magazine

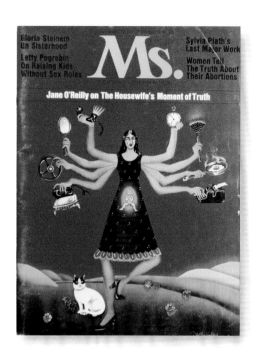

has evolved to address moms dedicated to their careers, many of whom are their families' breadwinners, as well as moms who leave and reenter the workforce or start their own businesses. In 1986, the magazine launched its "Best Companies for Working Mothers" edition. Today owned by the Bonnier Corporation, *Working Mother* appeals to a wide variety of career-minded moms; in 2014, the magazine named Meghan Stabler as its first openly transgender Working Mother of the Year.

OPPOSITE President Jimmy Carter and his mother, Miss Lillian Carter, at the White House in February 1977, the month after he took office. **LEFT** *Working Mother* cover from July 1979. **ABOVE** The striking cover of *Ms.* magazine for spring 1972.

FUN FACT Famous writers who have published in *Ms.* magazine include Alice Walker, Angela Davis, and Susan Faludi.

Mom Fashions Through the Decades

F rom vacuuming in heels to sitting at a computer in yoga pants, moms have experienced a fashion evolution over the decades. Here is a gallery of the unique fashion trends mothers have had to contend with while managing their many roles and daily challenges.

The 1880s
Ruffles and bustles and flounces, oh my! Dresses of the 1880s were elaborate concoctions, with extra material gathered in the back, and lace and other extravagant features adding to the look. Underskirts and petticoats gave the dresses extra texture. Imagine chasing after toddlers wearing all that fabric! This image from the February 1888 issue of *Peterson's*, an American magazine for women, showed the latest Paris fashions suitable for "afternoon callers."

The 1900s
The turn of the century witnessed some elaborate and constrictive women's fashions, such as a corset that gave women an *S* shape (pushing the bosom out and the hips back), as depicted in this corset ad from *Ladies' Home Journal*, October 1900. Toward the end of the century, thankfully, a more tailored look emerged, freeing women from the cumbersome layers and frills.

The 1920s

The Roaring Twenties generally calls to mind flappers in dresses without waistlines, adorned by strings of beads. While Mom probably wasn't out shimmying around the jazz club, she did enjoy a bit more freedom in shorter, less-constrictive skirts like the one worn by the mother in this illustration on the October 1929 *Good Housekeeping* cover.

The 1910s

The "New Woman" had a scaled-down, simpler style. While the frills were largely gone, the hobble skirt became popular—with a narrow hem that made walking difficult. Two such styles from 1911 are seen here from a publication called *American Dressmaker*. Fortunately for Mom, this style was short-lived, eventually giving way to the more practical full skirt.

The 1930s

Clothing was classic and feminine, with natural waistlines. Tailored suits and sleeveless blouses were popular as well. This illustration of a mother and daughter is from a 1931 catalog.

The 1940s

With rationing and many women entering the workforce during World War II, fashions were heavily influenced by the simple, practical work clothes of the time. Tailored suits and skirts just below the knee were popular, and sometimes Mom even wore pants, like this mom from Detroit photographed with her children in 1942.

The 1950s

The '50s saw a return to a soft, feminine look, with narrow waistlines, full skirts, and often sleeveless dresses. Skirts and blouses were also common, like the combo worn by this housewife shopping at a grocery store in 1957, and the pants trend became more popular than ever.

The 1960s

Mom could follow hippie counterculture fashion, model her style after the elegant Jackie Kennedy, or throw on a blouse and pair of pants. And then, of course, there was the bouffant, worn elegantly by this mom in Albany, New York, in 1969.

The 1970s

The '70s mom had it made—she could carry out her daily tasks in pants! Of course, those pants were often bell-bottoms, but they were comfortable nonetheless. This mom is outfitted in a chic matching pants and sleeveless top ensemble in 1970 in Upstate New York.

The 1990s

Who could forget the signature "mom jeans" of the '90s? With their unflattering proportions, these casual pants may not have been Mom's best look—although it is one of the most memorable.

The 1980s

Everything was bold in the '80s, from big hair and high-tops to brightly colored eyeshadow and velour pants. Here the author poses with her mother—who sports a T-shirt declaring "A man's house is his castle. Let him clean it!"—in 1984 near New York City.

The 2000s

Moms of the new millennium are all about comfort when they're at home. Since the arrival of the twenty-first century, Mom has chauffeured her kids to play dates and soccer practice in casual gear from tracksuits to yoga pants. While she may not be doing any actual yoga, the fashion is freeing—and a far cry from the corsets of her great-grandmother's day.

TEN

Rise of the Supermom

"A mother's love, while demonstrated daily in acts of tenderness and generosity, is always a source of wonder. . . . Her devotion never fails to fill us with gratitude and awe."

—President George H. W. Bush

A MERICA IN THE '80s was a time of both conservatism and innovation. Families frequented video arcades, the computer was named *Time* magazine's 1982 "Man of the Year," the Berlin Wall came down, and the Fox and MTV networks were launched. The American mother was changing as well: According to the Bureau of Labor Statistics, in the '80s, mothers working outside the home were "more the rule than the exception." Women were opting for smaller families, beginning motherhood at later ages, and making significant contributions to the family income. Single-parent households were becoming more prominent and accepted. These changes were mirrored in the TV shows, ads, books, and media of the time, depicting moms doing it all. The sky was literally the limit as one mother prepared to travel into space. In the '80s—with her happy family, big ambitions, and even bigger hair—there was nothing Mom couldn't do.

OPPOSITE Phylicia Rashad as Claire Huxtable on *The Cosby Show*—attorney, wife, and mother of five, she was one of the most iconic TV supermoms of the 1980s.

Supermoms of the Small Screen

Sitcoms of the '80s saw an influx of high-powered career moms—often in previously male professions—who succeeded at work and at home, were happily married (or in some cases contentedly single), and spent quality time with their children. Their kids' problems were cleverly solved in half an hour, their bosses were placated, and somehow their homes weren't overflowing with toys and laundry. It was fantasy television at its finest.

Perhaps the most famous sitcom mom of the '80s was Clair Huxtable, played by Phylicia Rashad, on *The Cosby Show* (1984–92) (see page 122). Clair was an attorney, mother of five children, and a doctor's wife. As the matriarch of an upper-middle-class African American family in Brooklyn, she kept her kids in line, maintained the romance with her husband, and found time to host intergenerational dinners—all without breaking a sweat. On *Family Ties* (1982–89), Elyse Keaton, played by Meredith Baxter-Birney, was a married architect raising three children (with a fourth who arrived later), who pursued interests including singing and trying to maintain her '60s liberal ideals in an era of Reagan trickle-down economics.

Several sitcoms of the time portrayed parents in gender reversals. On *Who's the Boss?* (1984–92), Angela Bower (Judith Light) was a divorced advertising executive who hired Tony Micelli (Tony Danza), a single father, to be her live-in housekeeper and take care of the home and her son while she worked. And on *Growing Pains* (1985–92), in the first episode Maggie Malone Seaver (Joanna Kerns) went back to work as a journalist, and her husband, Jason Seaver (Alan Thicke), moved his psychiatric practice into the home to care for the children in her absence.

As a sign of the times, Maggie's young son asks her, "Mommy, why did you have to go back to work?" And she answers him honestly, "I didn't 'have to.' I wanted to." Moms had reached a point where it wasn't shameful to want a career—nor was there any shame in fathers being more involved in caring for their children or the home.

OPPOSITE, TOP The *Growing Pains*' Seavers see mom Maggie (Joanna Kerns) off to work: Kirk Cameron (son Mike), Alan Thicke (stay-at-home dad and psychiatrist Jason), Jeremy Miller (son Ben), and Tracey Gold (daughter Carol). **OPPOSITE, BOTTOM** Alyssa Milano (the housekeeper's daughter, Samantha Micelli), Judith Light (working mom Angela Bower), and Tony Danza (housekeeper Tony Micelli) in a scene from *Who's the Boss*. **ABOVE** Phylicia Rashad shares a moment on *The Cosby Show* with Keshia Knight Pulliam, who played the youngest Huxtable daughter, Rudy.

FUN FACT When *The Cosby Show* was first pitched to NBC, the Huxtables were a blue-collar couple, with Clair written as a plumber.

Of course, this idyllic view of the balanced, supportive family left room for shows about families that weren't so perfect. On *Roseanne* (1988–97), Roseanne Barr played a working-class mom who often fought with her daughters and husband, and whose family struggled to get by. And then there was *Married . . . with Children* (1987–97), a comedy that parodied the traditional family sitcom, starring Katey Sagal as the lazy, brassy mother, Peggy Bundy—everything the polished, hardworking moms of '80s sitcoms were not. As the '90s approached, and women grew exhausted from trying to have it all, the veneer of the '80s supermom began to fade, and more realistic portrayals were to come.

ABOVE The Bundy clan from the satiric *Married . . . with Children*: David Faustino (son Bud), Ed O'Neill (dad Ed), Katey Sagal (Mom Peggy), Christina Applegate (daughter Kelly). **RIGHT** Roseanne Barr's portrayal of audacious "domestic goddess" Roseanne Connor helped propel *Roseanne* to the #1 US television show in the late '80s. Here, the Connor family: Lecy Goranson (daughter Becky), John Goodman (dad Dan), Barr (Roseanne), Sara Gilbert (Darlene), and Michael Fishman (D.J.). **OPPOSITE** A frazzled-looking Michael Keaton in a scene from the 1983 film *Mr. Mom*.

Mr. Mom (1983)

The '80s were known for their sitcom moms who were also powerhouses in the career world. Ambitious moms were found on the big screen as well, such as in the hit 1987 film *Baby Boom*. When career woman J. C. Wiatt (Diane Keaton) suddenly finds herself caring for a late cousin's baby, her life turns upside down—and she emerges as a loving mom and successful entrepreneur. But what happens when an '80s dad tries to take over a traditional mom's role? In the 1983 comedy film *Mr. Mom*, Jack (Michael Keaton), having recently lost his job, becomes a stay-at-home dad to three children while his wife, Caroline (Teri Garr), enters the full-time workforce as an advertising executive. Hilarity ensues as Jack attempts to change diapers, tame household appliances gone wild, and take on the local housewives in coupon poker. This gender-bending film proves that there's nothing easy about parenting—no matter who earns the income.

"My mother had a good deal of trouble with me, but I think she enjoyed it."

—*Mark Twain*

Famous Sitcom Kids

Everyone knows that sitcom moms are nothing without their youthful sidekicks. The most famous moms of the '80s had some of the most famous—and sometimes challenging—kids on television. Maggie Seaver had to contend with her son Mike (Kirk Cameron, see photograph on page 124), a teenage lothario who was frequently getting into trouble. And if that wasn't enough, the show cast Leonardo DiCaprio as Luke Bower, a homeless teen taken in by the Seaver clan. Similarly, Elyse Keaton was often at odds with her conservative Republican son, Alex P. Keaton (Michael J. Fox), as well as her sometimes materialistic daughter Mallory (Justine Bateman). And while Samantha Micelli (Alyssa Milano) wasn't exactly a problem child, raising a young girl was often challenging for the former professional baseball player Tony, requiring Angela Bower to lend a motherly hand.

Of course, these feisty teens were no match for the '80s supermom. Clair Huxtable managed five difficult children, including characters played by Lisa Bonet and Malcolm-Jamal Warner, who broke rules, argued, and occasionally required Clair to intervene with her legal prowess. But through it all, these TV moms were calm, patient, and wise—the perfect TV role models for the not-so-perfect TV children.

OPPOSITE, TOP On *Who's the Boss*, divorced mom Angela Bower often steps in to offer maternal support to Samantha Micelli, played with spunky appeal by a young Alyssa Milano. OPPOSITE, BOTTOM Four of the five headstrong Huxtable children from *The Cosby Show*—(from left) Tempestt Bledsoe as Vanessa, Keshia Knight Pulliam as Rudy, Lisa Bonet as Denise, and Malcolm-Jamal Warner as Theo. ABOVE On *Family Ties*, the two eldest children—staunch conservative Alex (played by Michael J. Fox, far right) and self-centered Mallory (Justine Bateman, seated, left)—clashed with their counterculture parents Steven and Elyse (Michael Gross and Meredith Baxter-Birney (standing, left).

Nelle Reagan

Mother of Ronald Reagan

Born in Fulton, Illinois, in 1883, Nelle Clyde Wilson was the oldest of seven children. She married her husband, Jack Reagan, in 1904, and the couple went on to have two children, Neil and Ronald. The family moved around a lot, often struggling for money, eventually settling in Dixon, Illinois, when Ronald was nine.

Nelle was active in her church, giving Bible readings and leading Sunday school services. Not surprisingly, given her son's later career as an actor, she also wrote and acted in community plays. After moving to California, Ronald bought his parents a house in Hollywood. After Jack died in 1941, Nelle volunteered at a local prison and a tuberculosis sanitarium in California, making weekly visits to offer encouragement and support to prisoners and patients alike. Nelle Reagan died in 1962 at age seventy-nine.

"There is no love like a mother's . . . she who gives of her heart and soul and self for the good and the happiness of her children and her family."

—*President Ronald Reagan*

Christa McAuliffe and the Challenger

One of the most famous mothers of the '80s was also at the center of one of the decade's most tragic events. In 1984, President Reagan announced the Teachers in Space program, in which NASA sought to fly an educator into space to communicate with students from orbit. New Hampshire teacher Christa McAuliffe was chosen from more than eleven thousand applicants—the first American civilian selected to go into space. While in orbit, McAuliffe planned to teach lessons to be broadcast to millions of schoolchildren, as well as conduct experiments in the fields of hydroponics, magnetism, and more. A goal of the program was to help kids understand space and the American space program.

McAuliffe boarded the *Challenger* spacecraft in Cape Canaveral, Florida, on January 28, 1986, along with six other crewmembers. As children nationwide watched on televisions in their classrooms, the shuttle broke apart seventy-three seconds into its flight, leaving no survivors and a devastated nation to mourn. The tragedy was later attributed to a design flaw.

Christa McAuliffe was born in 1948 in Boston, Massachusetts, the oldest of five children. She became an American history teacher in Maryland in 1970, later earning her master's degree and moving to Concord, New Hampshire, with her husband, Steven McAuliffe. The couple had two children, who were ages six and nine when their mother died. After her death, Christa McAuliffe was awarded the Congressional Space Medal of Honor, and has inspired the names of various landmarks in space, including the asteroid 3352 McAuliffe, the crater McAuliffe on the moon, and a crater on the planet Venus.

"I touch the future. I teach."

—*Christa McAuliffe*

OPPOSITE Ronald Reagan poses with his mother, Nelle, during his service with the First Motion Picture Unit in California, during World War II. **RIGHT** Christa McAuliffe during a training session at Johnson Space Center, Houston, in preparation for the *Challenger* flight, December 17, 1985.

Writing the Book on Mom

Mothers in the '80s didn't just dominate the small screen. Bestselling novels depicted the complexities of mother-daughter relationships. Amy Tan's *The Joy Luck Club*, published in 1989, told the multigenerational story of Chinese immigrant mothers and their American-born daughters. The critically acclaimed story, in which the women gather in San Francisco to play mah-jongg and trade stories that span decades and continents, illustrates the depth of love and forgiveness that exists between mothers and daughters.

Similarly, in Mona Simpson's bestselling 1986 novel *Anywhere But Here*, a mother and daughter drive from Wisconsin to Los Angeles with ambitions of wealth and a life in show business, following an unexpected path of love, fantasy, and unfulfilled expectations. And in Toni Morrison's Pulitzer Prize–winning novel *Beloved*, published in 1987, mother-daughter relationships are explored in the context of slavery, sacrifice, and the African American experience.

All three of these novels were adapted into feature films. *The Joy Luck Club* (opposite, bottom) came out in 1993, *Anywhere But Here* (starring Susan Sarandon and Natalie Portman) in 1999, and *Beloved* (starring Oprah Winfrey, Danny Glover, and Thandie Newton) in 1998.

OPPOSITE, TOP Author Amy Tan, 2008. **OPPOSITE, BOTTOM** The actresses who portrayed the mothers and daughters of the 1993 movie adaptation of Amy Tan's *The Joy Luck Club*: Kieu Chinh, Ming-Na Wen, Tamlyn Tomita, Tsai Chin, France Nuyen, Lauren Tom, Lisa Lu, and Rosalind Chao. **ABOVE** Novelist Mona Simpson at the Miami Book Fair International, 2014. **LEFT** Pulitzer and Nobel Prize–winning author Toni Morrison, during a lecture at West Point Military Academy in March 2013.

ELEVEN

Mommy Tracked

"Mothers are not only our life-givers, but they are also our nurturers
who sustain us with deep and unconditional love."

—President Bill Clinton

THE 1990s SAW great strides in technology and scientific advancement, with the development of the World Wide Web, advances in cloning and stem cell research, and more. Prosperity and controversy framed the decade, with the inauguration and impeachment of Bill Clinton. There was a greater focus on the individual, and TV shows reveled in single life, with shows like *Friends*, *Seinfeld*, *Ally McBeal*, and *The Real World* dominating the small screen. And yet family life still sparked discussion, centering on challenges faced by working mothers, both at home and at work itself, with the "mommy track" becoming a controversial topic.

Despite longer hours spent at work, the amount of time mothers spent on childcare rose in the '90s, with college-educated mothers increasing childcare time by more than nine hours per week, paving the way for modern-day "helicopter moms."

OPPOSITE Moms continued to swell the American workforce in the 1990s, fueling continued debates about whether women could "do it all"—successfully balance family life and a career.

Giving Her All

Despite the power sitcom moms of the '80s, who expertly balanced career and family, by the late '80s and early '90s the discussion had started to shift to a new question: Could Mom really do it all? Magazines and newspapers ran stories about successful, professional women leaving the workforce and retreating into the domestic sphere. A 1986 *Fortune* magazine cover read "Why Women Are Bailing Out." In 1988, the idea of the "mommy track" was introduced in the *New York Times* by journalist Jennifer A. Kingson, reporting about the lack of professional advancement experienced by mothers who were associates at law firms. In 1990, *Newsweek* ran an article "Mommy vs. Mommy," introducing the idea of the "mommy wars," pitting working mother against stay-at-home mother in a hostile feud over each other's differing choices. In response, a new wave of feminist bestsellers tackled the issues faced by women and mothers, such as Susan Faludi's *Backlash* (1991) and Marilyn French's *The War Against Women* (1992). Tensions were running high, and Mom was in the middle.

In response, television sitcoms ran the gamut, from more traditional stay-at-home moms (*Everybody Loves Raymond*) to single working moms (*Sister, Sister*) to unconventional mother stand-ins (*The Nanny*)—even a mom who went from a career-minded direction to a more traditional one with a change of season and cast (*The Fresh Prince of Bel-Air*). Famous '50s and '60s moms Shirley Jones, Marion Ross, and Florence Henderson were featured in a 1998 "Got Milk?" ad. Even the decade's First Ladies—Barbara Bush and Hillary Clinton—couldn't be more different. It was a transitional time, and one that showed many dimensions, joys, and challenges of motherhood.

LEFT The cast of *The Fresh Prince of Bel-Air*: front, from left—Tatyana Ali, James Avery, Will Smith; back—Karyn Parsons, Joseph Marcell, Janet Hubert, Alfonso Ribeiro. RIGHT *The Nanny* star Fran Drescher (as "Nanny" Fran Fine) with her charges; Madeline Zima (Grace Sheffield), Nicholle Tom (Maggie Sheffield), and Benjamin Salisbury (Brighton Sheffield).

FUN FACT On *The Fresh Prince of Bel-Air*, mother and aunt Vivian "Viv" Banks was played by two different actresses over the course of the show. During the first three seasons she was played by Janet Hubert as an outspoken career woman with a PhD. In the final three seasons, she was played by Daphne Maxwell-Reid as a more traditional homemaker.

Barbara Bush

Mother of George W. Bush

Barbara Bush, née Barbara Pierce, was born in Flushing, New York, in 1925. She grew up in Rye in New York's Westchester County before attending boarding school in South Carolina. She met her future husband, George Bush, when she was only sixteen years old at a dance during her Christmas vacation. A year and a half later the two became engaged, and George left to serve in the navy. After he returned on leave, she left Smith College, and the couple married in 1945.

After the war, Barbara and George Bush went to live in Texas, and had six children: George, Robin, Jeb, Neil, Marvin, and Dorothy. George worked in the oil industry, and eventually turned to politics, serving as a congressman, ambassador, and vice president. As Second Lady of the United States (the wife of the vice president), she took up the cause of literacy, continuing her advocacy as First Lady and becoming honorary chairman of the Barbara Bush Foundation for Family Literacy. She has volunteered with many causes, including outreach to the homeless and elderly.

The mother of two-term president George W. Bush and former Florida governor Jeb Bush, Barbara Bush today lives in Houston, Texas.

"I may be the only mother in America who knows exactly what their child is up to all the time."

—*Barbara Bush*

Musical Mamas

While '80s girls just wanted to have fun, in the '90s many icons of the music industry were singing the praises of motherhood, and began having children. Cyndi Lauper—the creator of the infamous party-girl anthem herself—gave birth to son Declyn Wallace Thornton in 1997. Madonna, the '80s pop star known for her unique couture and redefining boundaries, found a softer image when she gave birth to her daughter Lourdes Maria Ciccone Leon in 1996—the inspiration for Madonna's song "Little Star" (*Ray of Light*). Superstar Lauryn Hill also first became a mother in the '90s. The former *As the World Turns* actress and Fugees singer gave birth to son Zion David in 1997, recounting the experience in her hit song "To Zion" (*The Miseducation of Lauryn Hill*). And in 1992, famous grunge couple Courtney Love—the lead singer of Hole—and Nirvana front man Kurt Cobain gave birth to a baby girl, Frances Bean Cobain.

Mommy Mix Tape

Moms in the '90s worked hard, but at least they were appreciated! Here are some songs from the '90s and 2000s that are all about Mom.

- "Mama, I'm Coming Home" (1991) – Ozzy Osbourne
- "You Can't Lose Me" (1995) – Faith Hill
- "Dear Mama" (1995) – 2Pac (Tupac Shakur)
- "Mama" (1996) – Spice Girls
- "Mama Said" (1996) – Metallica
- "A Song for Mama" (1997) – Boyz II Men
- "The Perfect Fan" (1999) – The Backstreet Boys
- "I Love My Momma" (1999) – Snoop Dogg
- "Thank You, Mom" (2000) – Good Charlotte
- "Oh Mother" (2006) – Christina Aguilera
- "Mama's Song" (2009) – Carrie Underwood

OPPOSITE First Lady Barbara Bush, a tireless advocate for literacy, reads to children in the White House Library, July 1990. **ABOVE** Madonna and her first daughter, Lourdes, in New York City, April 1998.

Movie Moms—Modern Favorites

For film fans who enjoy a good ugly cry, modern cinema is filled with emotional and often heartbreaking stories of mother-child drama. Perhaps the most famous of these is *Terms of Endearment* (1983), starring mother-daughter duo Aurora (Shirley MacLaine) and Emma (Debra Winger). The Academy Award–winning film follows their relationship through the highs and lows of their lives—from marriage and children to adultery and cancer—that alternately push them apart and pull them close together. Equally emotional is the 1998 film *Stepmom*, starring Susan Sarandon and Julia Roberts as the embattled mother and soon-to-be stepmother of two children who struggle with knowing where their loyalties should lie. The film, which acknowledges the important role of stepparents, takes an emotional turn when Susan Sarandon's character grows sick, proving that children can never have too many people who love them.

An inspirational modern hit is *Akeelah and the Bee* (2006), the story of eleven-year-old Akeelah (Keke Palmer), a girl from South Los Angeles who participates in the Scripps National Spelling Bee. While her mother, Tanya (Angela Bassett)—a widowed mom struggling to make ends meet—is initially skeptical of her daughter's involvement in the bee, she soon becomes one of her biggest supporters and is inspired by her daughter's dedication. And for laughter and tears alike, the

2004 film *Spanglish* stars Paz Vega as a Mexican mother supporting her daughter by working for a wealthy LA family—and trying to keep her daughter close in a world where things aren't always what they seem.

From sentimental dramas to romantic comedies, today's films continue to celebrate Mom—a fan favorite who never goes out of style.

"A mother holds her children's hands for a while, their hearts forever."

—*Author unknown*

OPPOSITE Shirley MacLaine and Debra Winger as mother Aurora and daughter Emma in the heart-wrenching 1983 film *Terms of Endearment*, which won five Academy Awards, including Best Picture, Best Actress (MacLaine), and Best Director (James L. Brooks). **ABOVE** Angela Bassett and Keke Palmer in a scene from the inspirational *Akeelah and the Bee*, 2006. **RIGHT** Paz Vega and Victoria Luna in the 2004 mother-daughter film *Spanglish*, also directed by James L. Brooks.

TWELVE

Moms in Cyberspace

THE NEW MILLENNIUM

*"Mothers who protect, teach, and nurture their children with all their hearts
strengthen their families and help build a better future for our country."*

—President George W. Bush

W ITH THE ADVENT of social media, motherhood has captured the imagination—and often outrage—of parents and non-parents around the world,
leading to instantaneous debates among millions about everything from where baby
sleeps to the proper age to cease breastfeeding. It's also led to far-flung communities of
mothers able to share—through Facebook, videos, blog posts, and more—everything
from recipes to baby sleep secrets to kid-friendly craft ideas. With telecommuting,
lines between working and stay-at-home mothers continue to blur, as moms work from
home or pursue part-time freelance gigs, sometimes writing and monetizing blogs aimed
at other moms. Reflecting the changing times, movies and television portray a greater
diversity of families, featuring same-sex, adoptive, and other nontraditional families.

OPPOSITE Mothers and children in the twenty-first century—the age of social media—communicate with each
other, with other mothers, and with the world at large in previously unimaginable ways.

ABOVE Sheryl Sandberg, the COO of Facebook and founder of LeanIn.org, at a press conference in Tokyo to discuss the Japanese edition of her book, *Lean In* (2013). **OPPOSITE** Readers on the Internet are constantly debating the right ways to feed a baby—including where it's appropriate to nurse, when to wean, or whether baby should have breast or bottle.

> "The trouble with being a parent is that by the time you are experienced, you are unemployed."
>
> —*Anonymous*

The twenty-first-century American mom has emerged as a new woman, refusing to conform to conventional roles, sharing her experiences worldwide, and, above all, keeping her children at the center of her world.

Mother Knows Best?

Social media has a way of attracting diverse opinions, and when it comes to motherhood, it seems everyone has something to say. Today there is no shortage of issues inviting comments: helicopter moms versus free-range moms, bottle-feeding versus breast, public versus private breastfeeding, cry it out versus co-sleeping, stay-at-home moms versus working moms, and a host of other issues from when to give kids a smartphone to how best to discipline unruly children. Internet comment sections have become spaces for both support and "mom-shaming," for thoughtful discussions and heated disputes. And the Internet's laser-sharp focus isn't restricted to parents updating their status or commenting on school dress codes—online debate has raged about everything from how many children the Duke and Duchess of Cambridge should have to where the Obama daughters should go to school.

So-called "experts" can't agree on many parenting issues, either. Magazines and books weigh in with conflicting advice, from a 2012 article in the *Atlantic* positing "Why Women Still Can't Have It All" to Facebook executive Sheryl

Sandberg advising women to "lean in" to their careers. And, while many books and articles promote the idea of "breast is best," *Time* magazine shocked viewers with its May 21, 2012, cover depicting a woman breastfeeding her three-year-old son. Exploring the concept of attachment parenting—a parenting method emphasizing physical closeness and touch—the *Time* cover boldly asked "Are You Mom Enough?" For many outraged readers, the answer was a resounding "no, thank you."

FUN FACT Famous moms who've practiced or supported attachment parenting include Mayim Bialik, Alicia Silverstone, P!nk, and Alanis Morissette.

Ann Dunham

Mother of Barack Obama

Stanley Ann Dunham was born in 1942 in Wichita, Kansas. Her father was in the army, and after World War II the family moved to California, Oklahoma, Texas, and Kansas, before settling in Seattle, Washington, where Dunham attended high school. In 1959, the family moved to Hawaii, and Dunham attended the University of Hawaii at Mānoa, where she met Barack Obama Sr., an economist from Kenya. In 1961, the couple married, and Dunham gave birth to Barack Obama II at the age of eighteen.

When her husband left for Harvard, Dunham's parents helped her raise her young son, Barack. The couple divorced in 1964; in 1965, Dunham married Lolo Soetoro (whom she eventually divorced) and gave birth to a daughter a few years later. Dunham earned her master's and PhD in anthropology and conducted fieldwork in Indonesia, leaving Barack to finish high school in Hawaii while living with his grandparents. In addition to her work in anthropology, during her life she taught English, worked in rural development, briefly took up residence in Pakistan, and lived and worked in Indonesia. Ann Dunham died of cancer in 1995.

"[My mother] was somebody who was hungry for adventure and skeptical of convention. But she loved the heck out of her kids. . . . There was never a moment where I didn't feel as if I was special."

—*President Barack Obama*

Mom Goes Viral

The twenty-first century has given moms their own voice, in the form of blogs, social media, videos, and more. Moms share their experiences, parenting tips, and more online, often using their reach to monetize their blogs and other online content. Working with brands as "influencers" to recommend the latest stroller or gluten-free line of snacks to other parents, stay-at-home and working moms alike are able to earn extra income from their laptops, often collaborating and networking with other "mom bloggers" around the world. Some publications, such as the *Huffington Post*, the *Washington Post*, and the *New York Times*, have formed their own highly successful online parenting sections, where writers and bloggers can contribute to the ongoing dialogue about modern parenting. Other sites offer a more humorous, unfiltered view of motherhood, such as Scary Mommy, or speak to the experiences of certain demographics, such as fathers or Jewish parents.

Topics discussed on these blogs vary widely, from tear-jerking odes to the fleeting nature of toddlerhood to intimate accounts of divorce and substance abuse to entertaining gossip about celebrity parents. Running the gamut from humorous to confessional, these posts are sometimes shared hundreds of thousands of times on social media—bringing mothers' personal stories to a global parenting community.

ABOVE Many stay-at-home and working moms alike blog about motherhood, writing on a wide range of topics and networking with other moms and "mom bloggers" around the world. **OPPOSITE** Ann Dunham in Jakarta with her son, Barack Obama (right); her second husband, Lolo Soetoro (left); and baby daughter Maya Soetoro, Obama's half sister, c. 1971.

> "We are millions of unique women, united by motherhood. We are scary, and we are proud."
>
> —*Scary Mommy*

BY THE NUMBERS
According to a survey by BabyCenter® in 2014, one in five millennial moms has started a blog with "substantial followers."

> "The family is
> one of nature's
> masterpieces."
>
> —*George Santayana*

The New Face of Family

With social media bringing so many different voices to the parenting conversation, it's not surprising that this diversity has spread to other areas of pop culture as well. Twenty-first-century television has featured adoptive, same-sex, interracial, and culturally diverse parents on popular television shows such as *Grey's Anatomy*, *Modern Family*, and more. On *Parenthood* (2010–15), Crosby (Dax Shepard) and Jasmine (Joy Bryant) were an interracial couple raising a son, while Crosby's sister Julia (Erika Christensen) and her husband, Joel (Sam Jaeger), adopted a Latino boy whose mom was incarcerated. On *Grey's Anatomy* (2005), Meredith Grey (Ellen Pompeo) and her husband, Derek Shepherd (Patrick Dempsey), adopted a baby girl from Malawi; their same-sex colleagues Callie (Sara Ramirez) and Arizona (Jessica Capshaw) raised a baby together. On *This Is Us* (2016), young parents Rebecca (Mandy Moore) and Jack (Milo Ventimiglia) turned their newborn twins into triplets when they adopted an African American baby boy who had been abandoned by his birth father at a fire station.

On the sitcom *Modern Family* (2009), Colombia-born Gloria Pritchett (Sofia Vergara) is the wife of Jay (Ed O'Neill), the older patriarch of the Pritchett family, and mother of Manny and, later, Joe. A stay-at-home mom, she is traditional and proud of her heritage—in addition to being loud, outspoken, and devoted to her family, which includes the nuclear and same-sex families of her husband's children. Known for her distinct voice, fiery temper, and big heart, Gloria is part of a modern family that represents a new direction in American television.

The diverse modern American family can also be found in advertisements. According to a 2016 report from BabyCenter, 80 percent of parents say they like seeing diverse families in ads. The report—which spotlighted households with parents who were single, cohabiting, LGBTQ, mixed race, or that included stay-at-home dads—advised advertisers to depict diverse families authentically and realistically, and highlight universal truths and experiences that all families share.

OPPOSITE *Modern Family*'s Sofia Vergara as Gloria Delgado-Pritchett; Ed O'Neill as her second husband, Jay Pritchett; and Rico Rodriguez as Gloria's son from a previous marriage, Manny Delgado.

BY THE NUMBERS
According to the 2016 survey by BabyCenter, millennials especially value diversity. Forty-nine percent of millennial parents are more likely to discuss products with their friends if the ads include diverse family types—and 41 percent are more likely to buy these products.

STAGE MOMS

All the world's a stage—and when Mom is acting on it, audiences listen. From sharp-witted comedies to heartrending dramas, for years mothers have been inspiring theatergoers from Broadway to community theaters. Here are just a few mothers who've lit up the stage.

Lost Mom: Kate Keller, *All My Sons*
In this award-winning play written by Arthur Miller—which opened on Broadway in 1947, directed by Elia Kazan—Kate Keller lives in denial. She refuses to accept that her son Larry, who went missing several years earlier in World War II, is gone—or that her husband knowingly shipped damaged airplane parts to the military, causing the deaths of twenty-one pilots. When Larry's girlfriend and her brother return to the Keller household, truths emerge and Kate's life is changed forever. This beloved play has been revived many times, including a 2008 Broadway production that starred Dianne Wiest, John Lithgow, and Katie Holmes.

Stage Mom: Mama (Madame) Rose, *Gypsy*
This 1959 musical, originally starring Ethel Merman, gave birth to the original "stage mom." Loosely based on the memoirs of burlesque artist Gypsy Rose Lee, the show, written by Arthur Laurents, with music and lyrics by Jule Styne and Stephen Sondheim, follows ambitious Rose as she attempts to force show business careers on her young daughters, June and Louise. A complex look at a mother chasing her own dreams through her children, it's a powerful statement about a mother's influence—and what happens when children grow beyond it.

Drag Mom: Edna Turnblad, *Hairspray*

Based on the 1988 film by John Waters, this 2003 Tony Award winner for Best Musical brought audiences the plus-sized and ever-supportive Edna Turnblad. Edna's big-haired daughter Tracy longs for a place on a '60s Baltimore dance show, *The Corny Collins Show.* Edna helps Tracy follow her dream of performing on and racially integrating the show, even bailing out those marching against the station after they're all arrested. Originally played by Harvey Fierstein, Edna is an unusual mother—with a heart of gold.

Bad Mom: Violet Weston, *August: Osage County*

Tracy Letts's Pulitzer Prize– and Tony Award– winning show opened in 2007, first in Chicago and then on Broadway. A darkly comedic portrait of a dysfunctional family, *August: Osage County*

follows the family of Violet, the matriarch of the Weston family, as they attempt to help her through the sudden death of her husband. Addicted to prescription drugs and suffering from mouth cancer from years of smoking, Violet is the sharp-tongued mom audiences love to hate.

OPPOSITE Arthur Kennedy, Karl Malden, and Beth Merrill in the stage production of *All My Sons*, 1947.
ABOVE LEFT *Gypsy* cast on Broadway in 1959; from left to right: Sandra Church as Rose's daughter Louise, Jack Klugman as manager Herbie, Jacqueline Mayro as Rose's daughter Baby June, Ethel Merman as ambitious stage mother Rose, and an unidentified actress.
ABOVE RIGHT Harvey Fierstein (as Edna Turnblad) performs a scene from the musical *Hairspray*, 2002.

Today's mom has come a long way from her nineteenth-century counterpart. While most mothers were never simply the "angel of the house," Mom's role has grown more complex over the years, offering choices and opportunities her predecessors couldn't imagine. And yet, the bond between a mother and her child remains unchanged. A tender smile, a warm embrace—these moments are the same whether Mom is in a petticoat, bell-bottoms, or yoga pants. From the first Mother's Day to modern-day depictions of mothers on the screen and stage, we continue to celebrate Mom, the ever-changing, always-loving heart of the American family.

Acknowledgments

A lot of people helped make this book a reality, starting with my own mother, Sandra Peters, who was my first introduction to the American mom. Somehow, while keeping the house spotless, all of us fed, and perpetually "balancing the checkbook" (whatever that means), she was always available to help me with my homework, support my afterschool activities, and encourage my writing. I'd also like to thank the first American dad in my life, my father, Dan Peters, who has always loved and supported me—and has clocked countless babysitting hours over the years. And, of course, none of this would have been possible without my husband, Chris Hale, planning activities and sitting through some truly terrible kids' movies so that I could have uninterrupted time to write. And I'm grateful to Sloane and Logan, who put up with Mommy disappearing into the office to write some book about something instead of playing another game of Go Fish or turning the new couch into a fort. You inspire me every day.

Giving birth to a book takes a village, and I couldn't have asked for a better one than Sterling Publishing. I'm grateful to the hard work and careful eye of my editor, Barbara Berger, who treats each of her books like her own baby, gently guiding its direction and addressing each imperfection with patience and kind words. She also convinced me I could write this book, and I'm continually thankful for her confidence in this project. I'd also like to thank Betsy Beier, Christine Heun, Linda Liang, Kayla Overbey, Fred Pagan, David Ter-Avanesyan, Theresa Thompson (with thanks also to Barbara Balch, layout designer), and the rest of the team at Sterling Publishing for their creative vision and support.

Notes and Further Reading

Chapter 1

Abbott, John S. C. *The Mother at Home; or, The Principles of Maternal Duty Familiarly Illustrated*. New York: Harper & Brothers, 1873. http://bit.ly/2waL6Mi.

Abbott, Karen. "Letters from Mothers to President Lincoln." *Smithsonian*. May 10, 2014. http://bit.ly/2xWFCt2.

Allen, S. S., Rev. C. Stone, and William C. Brown, eds. *The Mother's Assistant and Young Lady's Friend*. Boston: Cyrus Stone, 1853.

Child, Lydia Maria. *The Mother's Book*. Boston: Carter, Hendee and Babcock, 1831. http://bit.ly/2yfCog1.

"Gave War 16 Sons." *Montrose Daily Press* 3, no. 227 (March 3, 1911). http://bit.ly/2xrWshQ.

Hanc, John. "The History of the Christmas Card." *Smithsonian*. December 9, 2015. http://bit.ly/1SRbQWZ.

Handwerk, Brian. "Mother's Day Turns 100: Its Surprisingly Dark History." *National Geographic*. May 9, 2014. http://bit.ly/1mHGNwE.

History.com Staff. "Women in the Civil War." *History*. Accessed September 21, 2017. http://bit.ly/1Anoc09.

"Mary Peake." *History of American Women*. Accessed October 7, 2017. http://bit.ly/1P3pmF8.

Jamison, Dennis. "The Seeds of Mother's Day Were Planted During the Civil War." *Communities Digital News*. May 11, 2014. http://bit.ly/2wKOxZq.

MacLean, Maggie. "Mary Ann Bickerdyke." *Civil War Women*. August 23, 2008. http://bit.ly/2C3nLiZ.

Merelli, Annalisa. "How the Humble Greeting Card Continues to Thrive in the Digital Age." *Quartz*. December 23, 2016. http://bit.ly/2kF7lFm.

United Methodist News Service. "Mothers of U.S. Mother's Day Were West Virginia Methodists." *United Methodist Church News Service*. Accessed September 21, 2017. http://bit.ly/2wDfEut.

Esterberg, Kristin G. "Advice Literature for Mothers." In *Encyclopedia of Motherhood*, Vol. 1, edited by Andrea O'Reilly, 27–29. Thousand Oaks, CA: SAGE Publications, 2010. DOI: 10.4135/9781412979276.n11.

Smith, Ana Serafin. "Mother's Day Spending to Reach Record-High $23.6 Billion." *National Retail Federation*. April 24, 2017. http://bit.ly/2q7SaG3.

Tyler, Don. *Hit Songs, 1900–1955: American Popular Music of the Pre-Rock Era*. Jefferson, NC: McFarland & Company, 2007.

Chapter 2

Nudelman, Edward D. *Jessie Willcox Smith: American Illustrator*. Gretna, LA: Pelican Publishing Group, Inc., 1990.

Prieto, Laura R. *At Home in the Studio: The Professionalization of Women Artists in America*, 160. Cambridge, MA: Harvard University Press, 2001.

"The Red Rose Girls: An Uncommon Story of Art and Love." *USA Today*. May 2004. http://bit.ly/2fed42H.

Schiller, Joyce K. "Illustration Spurs Fashion—Fashion Spurs Illustration." Rockwell Center for American Visual Studies, Norman Rockwell Museum. May 14, 2014. http://bit.ly/2xrOPIk.

"Violet Oakley." Pennsylvania Capitol Preservation Committee. Accessed September 21, 2017. http://bit.ly/2kpM4PU.

Wheeler, Edward J., ed. "Mother-Love in Jessie Willcox Smith's Art." *Current Literature* XLV (July–December 2008): 635–641. http://bit.ly/2zHAkD8.

Chapter 3

Batchelor, Bob, ed. *American Pop: Popular Culture Decade by Decade*, Vol. 3, 1960–1989. Westport, CT: Greenwood Press, 2009.

Biagini, Antonello and Giovanna Motta. *The First World War: Analysis and Interpretation*. Vol. 1. Newcastle upon Tyne, UK: Cambridge Scholars Publishing, 2015.

Davis, Belinda. "The Mighty Women of World War I." CNN. Updated July 2, 2014. http://cnn.it/TDWoUZ.

Donson, Andrew. "Children and Youth." 1914–1918 *Online: International Encyclopedia of the First World War*, ed. by Ute Daniel, Peter Gatrell, Oliver Janz, Heather Jones, Jennifer Keene, Alan Kramer, and Bill Nasson, issued by Freie Universität Berlin, October 8, 2014. DOI: 10.15463/ie1418.10265.

Gilbert, Robert E. *The Mortal Presidency: Illness and Anguish in the White House*. New York: Fordham University Press, 1998.

Hampton, William Judson. *Our Presidents and Their Mothers*. Boston: Cornhill Publishing Company, 1922.

"History of the Blue Star Mothers of America, Inc." *Blue Star Mothers of America, Inc.* Accessed October 2, 2017. http://bit.ly/2nP7lYu.

Joiner, Mildred A. and Clarence M. Welner. "Employment of Women in War Production." *Bulletin*. Bureau of Employment Security. July 1942. http://bit.ly/2jP63Z6.

Kim, Tae H. "Where Women Worked During World War I." *Seattle General Strike Project*. Accessed September 21, 2017. http://bit.ly/2jP69Qs.

Tyler, Don. Music of the First World War. Santa Barbara, CA: ABC-CLIO, 2016.

Wasserman, Gary. "The Mama's Boys Who Became Our Presidents." *Washington Post*. May 12, 1985. http://wapo.st/2z1JZT8.

Chapter 4

Allen, Robert C. *Speaking of Soap Operas*. Chapel Hill: University of North Carolina Press, 1985.

Avey, Tori. "Who Was Betty Crocker?" *PBS Food*. February 15, 2013. http://to.pbs.org/2yg77tm.

Ciment, James. *Encyclopedia of the Jazz Age*. Vols. 1–2, *From the End of World War I to the Great Crash*. London: Routledge, 2015.

Cohen, Jennie. "The Mother Who Saved Suffrage: Passing the 19th Amendment." *History*. August 16, 2010. http://bit.ly/1oJY6Ca.

Commuri, Suraj, Ahmet Ekici, and Patricia Kennedy. "Historical Review of Advertising Targeting Mothers: Content Analysis Under Sociological Imagination of Ads in 1920s, 1950s, and 1980s," in *Advances in Consumer Research* 29 (2002): 114–23. http://bit.ly/2yfvhUN.

Drowne, Kathleen Morgan and Patrick Huber. American *Popular Culture Through History: The 1920s*. Ed. Ray B. Browne. Westport, CT: Greenwood Press, 2004.

Hall, Dennis and Susan G. Hall, eds. "Betty Crocker." In *American Icons*. Vol. 1. Westport, CT: Greenwood Press, 2006.

Hampton, William Judson. *Our Presidents and Their Mothers*. Boston: The Cornhill Publishing Company, 1922.

Honey, Maureen. "Georgia Douglas Johnson's Life and Career." In *The Oxford Companion to African American Literature*, edited by William L. Andrews, Frances Smith Foster, and Trudier Harris, 403–4. New York: Oxford University Press, 1997.

Landau, Elaine. *Warren G. Harding*. Minneapolis: Lerner Publications Company, 2004.

Liccardo, Lynn. "Irna Phillips: Brief Life of Soap Opera's Single Mother: 1901–1973." *Harvard Magazine*. January–February 2013. http://bit.ly/2B58hNa.

Marks, Susan. *Finding Betty Crocker: The Secret Life of America's First Lady of Food*. New York: Simon & Schuster, 2005.

"Soap Operas during the Golden Age of Radio." *Old Time Radio Catalog*. Accessed October 2, 2017. http://bit.ly/2A9xhzB.

"The Story of Betty Crocker." *Betty Crocker*. Accessed October 2, 2017. http://bit.ly/2nPtdOR.

Chapter 5

Arbuckle, Alex Q. "1936: Migrant Mother." *Mashable*. Accessed October 2, 2017. http://on.mash.to/2AtQ9xA.

Ashley, Jeffrey S. *Betty Ford: A Symbol of Strength*. New York: Nova History Publications, 2003.

"First Lady Biography: Michelle Obama." *National First Ladies Library*. Updated February 5, 2009. http://bit.ly/2dIPU7L.

Roosevelt, Eleanor. "My Day, September 8, 1945," *The Eleanor Roosevelt Papers Digital Edition*. Accessed October 31, 2017. http://bit.ly/2BC0zLF.

"Roy Stryker and the FSA." *American Studies at the University of Virginia*. Last Modified May 10, 1999. https://at.virginia.edu/2Abj8C0.

Ware, Susan. "Women and the Great Depression." *History Now: The Journal of the Gilder Lehrman Institute*. Accessed October 16, 2017. http://bit.ly/1Gf1Rt5.

Chapter 6

"1940s War, Cold War and Consumerism." *Ad Age*. March 28, 2005. http://bit.ly/2o27uDv.

Cohen, Rhaina. "Who Took Care of Rosie the Riveter's Kids?" *The Atlantic*. November 18, 2015. http://theatln.tc/2jP84od.

"Dorothy Ducas Herzog Dies; Reporter, Editor and Author." *New York Times*. September 26, 1987. http://nyti.ms/2Au0QQS.

Goodwin, Doris Kearns. *No Ordinary Time: Franklin & Eleanor Roosevelt—The Home Front in World War II*. New York: Simon & Schuster, 1994.

Harvey, Sheridan. "Rosie the Riveter: Real Women Workers in World War II." Presentation transcript. Library of Congress. July 20, 2010. http://bit.ly/1IT0Yot.

Hershey, Lenore. *Between the Covers: The Lady's Own Journal*. New York: Coward-McCann, 1983.

Honey, Maureen. *Creating Rosie the Riveter: Class, Gender, and Propaganda During World War II*. Amherst: University of Massachusetts Press, 1984.

Langer, Emily. "Mary Doyle Keefe, Norman Rockwell's model for 'Rosie the Riveter,' dies at 92." *Washington Post*. April 23, 2015. http://wapo.st/2yfgEk8.

Novak, Matt. "Tomorrow's Kitchen (1943)." December 3, 2008. *Paleofuture*. http://bit.ly/2BAhWfW.

O'Brien, Kenneth Paul and Lynn H. Parsons, Eds. *The Home-Front War: World War II and American Society*. Westport, CT: Greenwood Press, 1995.

O'Connor, Aidan. "Kitchens of the Future." *Inside/Out: A MoMA/MoMA PS1 blog*. September 22, 2010. http://mo.ma/2B4ONbC.

"OWI Writer Finds She's Indispensable Only in Her Home." *Dunkirk Evening Observer*. December 8, 1943. http://bit.ly/2jOcifG.

"Sara Delano Roosevelt (1854–1941)." *The Eleanor Roosevelt Papers Project*. Accessed October 2, 2017. http://bit.ly/2z1KNXW.

Stoltzfus, Emilie. "Child Care: The Federal Role During World War II." *CRS Report for Congress. Domestic Social Policy Division*. Accessed December 7, 2017. http://bit.ly/1nk6U3d.

Chapter 7

Berman, Eliza. "Life Before Equal Pay Day: Portrait of a Working Mother in the 1950s." *Time*. April 13, 2015. http://ti.me/1JGMffl.

"Changes in men's and women's labor force participation rates." Bureau of Labor Statistics. January 10, 2017. http://bit.ly/2o4R7JE.

Cross, Amy. "A Humble Trailblazer: Meet Mary Alexander, the First African-American Woman to Appear in Coca-Cola Advertising." The Coca-Cola Company. April 12, 2013. http://bit.ly/2kn38pZ.

Edelstein, Sally. "The Real Housewives of the Cold War." *Envisioning the American Dream*. March 7, 2013. http://bit.ly/2Au1uhg.

Green, John and Alice Gomstyn. "'I Love Lucy' Voted the Best TV Show of All Time." *ABC News*. September 18, 2012. http://abcn.ws/2C3sz81.

"Historical Census of Housing Tables Ownership Rates." US Census Bureau. Last updated October 31, 2011. http://bit.ly/2C6mec4.

"'I Love Lucy,' 'Lucy Is Enceinte' More Than 60 Years Later and More Talked About TV Pregnancies." *Huffington Post*. Updated July 26, 2013. http://bit.ly/2iQJ5jj.

"Lucille Ball Adheres to Television Script; Comedienne Give Birth to 8½-Pound Boy." *New York Times*, January 20, 1953. http://nyti.ms/2AsmSTT.

Mintz, Steven and Susan Kellogg. *Domestic Revolutions: A Social History of American Family Life*. New York: The Free Press, 1988.

Muizz, Eirul. "Ritual and Ceremony: A History of Baby Showers." November 1, 2008. https://docuri.com/download/history-of-baby-showers_59c1dfedf581710b28697522_pdf.

Savage, Lesley. "Most Beloved Television Moms." *CBS News*. May 8, 2013. http://cbsn.ws/2Atqepz.

Weinraub, Bernard. "Dousing the Glow of TV's First Family: Time for the Truth About Ozzie and Harriet." *New York Times*. June 18, 1998. http://nyti.ms/2iFpaEl.

"'Women Are People, Too!': The Groundbreaking Article by Betty Friedan." *Good Housekeeping*. August 9, 2010. http://bit.ly/2jP7AOB.

Chapter 8

"Rose Fitzgerald Kennedy." John F. Kennedy Presidential Library and Museum. Accessed October 5, 2017. http://bit.ly/2kojbUt.

Walsh, Kenneth T. "The 1960s: A Decade of Change for Women." *US News & World Report*. March 12, 2010. http://bit.ly/2peaIr0.

"Women in the Labor Force." US Department of Labor. Last updated July 2016. http://bit.ly/2iTs4Fj.

Chapter 9

"Clothing." University of Vermont. Accessed October 5, 2017. http://bit.ly/2nQZhX1.

Evans, Charlotte. "Lillian Carter is Dead at 85; Mother of the 39th President." *New York Times*. October 31, 1983. http://nyti.ms/2yfvUO2.

"Feminism, Impact of." *Ad Age*. September 15, 2003. http://bit.ly/2B7MPai/.

Ford, Gerald. "Proclamation 4437–Mother's Day, 1976." The American Presidency Project. http://bit.ly/2jtLjce.

"Labor force participation rates 1975–2013." US Department of Labor. Accessed October 5, 2017. http://bit.ly/2BTWjmW.

Livingston, Gretchen and Anna Brown. "Birth rate for unmarried women declining for first time in decades." Pew Research Center. August 13, 2014. http://pewrsr.ch/2A9AnDJ /.

"Remarks by Selma Siegman Upon Acceptance of the YWCA's First 'International Woman of the Year Award' on Behalf of Miss Lillian Carter," pp. 52–53, Waldorf Astoria, New York, June 7, 1978. Jimmy Carter Library. http://bit.ly/2Atqoxb.

Schultz, E. J. "A Century of Women in Advertising." *Ad Age*. September 23, 2012. http://bit.ly/1wSaVjb.

Wang, Wendy, Kim Parker, and Paul Taylor. "Chapter 4: Single Mothers" in *Breadwinner Moms*. Pew Research Center. May 29, 2013. http://pewrsr.ch/1qaHmzc.

Chapter 10

Biography.com Editors. "Christa McAuliffe Biography.com." Biography.com. A&E Television Networks. Accessed October 7, 2017. http://bit.ly/2AbwHl4.

Bush, George H. W. "Proclamation 5974–Mother's Day, 1989." The American Presidency Project. http://bit.ly/2jP8WJb.

Grossman, Allyson Sherman. "Working Mothers and Their Children." *Monthly Labor Review: Special Labor Force Reports—Summaries*. May 1981. http://bit.ly/2B4XfaL.

"Faith and Ronald Reagan." *Reagan's Country*, Reagan Foundation Member Newsletter. March 2012. http://bit.ly/2z1DZK9.

Chapter 11

Black, Allida. "Barbara Pierce Bush." *The First Ladies of the United States of America.* The White House Historical Association, 2009. http://bit.ly/2BUazw7.

Clinton, William J. "Proclamation 6683—Mother's Day, 1994." The American Presidency Project. http://bit.ly/2kWqBSN.

Douglas, Susan A. and Meredith W. Michaels. "The Mommy Wars" in *The Mommy Myth,* 203–235. New York: The Free Press, 2004.

Kingson, Jennifer A. "Women in the Law Say Path Is Limited by 'Mommy Track.'" *New York Times*. August 8, 1988. http://nyti.ms/2C3DtKS.

Newsweek Staff. "Mommy vs. Mommy." *Newsweek*. June 3, 1990. http://bit.ly/1fYBxr4.

Ramey, Garey, Valerie A. Ramey, Erik Hurst, Daniel W. Sacks, and Betsey Stevenson. "The Rug Rat Race." *Brookings Papers on Economic Activity* (Spring 2010): 129-199. http://www.jstor.org/stable/40930483.

Chapter 12

"BabyCenter® Reveals Profile of Today's Millennial Mom: She's Resilient, Resourceful, Optimistic." BabyCenter. January 30, 2014. http://bit.ly/2Bzyogl.

"BabyCenter® & YouGov Research Reveals That Featuring Diverse Family Types In Advertising Resonates with Today's Parents." *PR Newswire*. March 7, 2016. http://prn.to/1Y187sm.

Bingham, Amy. "Five Unordinary Facts About President Obama's Mother." *ABC News*. May 12, 2012. http://abcn.ws/2hi5g4L.

Bush, George W. "Proclamation 7783—Mother's Day, 2004." The American Presidency Project. http://bit.ly/2Aae7tE.

Kenny, Caroline. "Obama Explains Why His Mom's Parenting Style Worked." CNN. December 28, 2016. http://cnn.it/2BezPjG.

Scary Mommy quote courtesy of Jill Smokler, founder. Scary Mommy. http://bit.ly/2iPh5g2.

President Barack Obama. *The Axe Files with David Axelrod*. CNN. December 26, 2016. http://www.cnn.com/2016/12/26/politics/axe-files-obama-transcript/index.html.

Picture Credits

Index

Note: Film and television characters are indexed under their first names.